NOT JUST A CIVIL SERVANT

NOT JUST A CIVIL SERVANT

Anil Swarup

UNICORN BOOKS

Unicorn Books Pvt. Ltd.
F-2/16, Ansari Road, Daryaganj, New Delhi-110002
• E-mail: info@unicornbooks.in

Edition: 2025
ISBN 978-81-7806-479-6 (Hard Bound)
ISBN 978-81-7806-480-2 (Paper Back)

Cover Design: PitchWorx

www.unicornbooks.in

Printed: Param Offsetters, Okhla, New Delhi-110020

Dedicated to my Parents

I am what I am because of them

Some Comments about the Book

An inspiring tale of what a few good officers can achieve despite the hurdles and red tape of India's soul killing bureaucracy. It confirms once again that the enemy of development is within. The book is written with honesty and passion by a person who worked all his life inside this callous system. I recommend it whole-heartedly.

Gurcharan Das, Author and Columnist

There are several superstars in the civil services, each deserving to be celebrated. But Anil Swarup is among those rare ones who are also powerful communicators of their ideas to wider audiences. I have, more than once, heard him speak to groups of younger bureaucrats on topics elucidated in the book. When he leaves the room, the listeners are left visibly charged with inspiration to do something out of the ordinary.

Unlike many other autobiographies of my colleagues in the civil service, Anil's book reads like a series of journalistic despatches of some of the better known accomplishments of his career in the IAS. Without unnecessary embellishment, his language touches you where it is intended to. The most amazing of the stories is about the conception, formulation and spreading out of the RSBY scheme. In my view, the book could as well have a subtitle, 'Serving the poorest of the poor'.

Prabhat Kumar, Former Cabinet Secretary and Former Governor, Jharkhand

Anil Swarup's destiny was carefully carved by his father the day he was born—to be an IAS officer. It is a destiny that took him places—from being a

Sub-Divisional Magistrate in Deoria, UP, overseeing the maximum number of passengers in vehicles, to being in the thick of a bank robbery shootout, featuring on the hitlist of Sikh terrorists, working and watching Kalyan Singh closely when the Babri mosque was demolished and navigating the Gangs of Wasseypur-style coal ministry. As he says in this book, government teaches you skills what they don't at Business School—like how to manage manufactured crises. The book passionately details his governance tour de force as he learnt how to douse communal tension, blow the whistle on 'speed money' in environment clearances and revived UP's moribund investment board. But what ultimately felt like a 'Bharat Ratna' moment for him was when he helped a man get back his job and prevented him from returning to a life of drugs.

Shekhar Gupta, Founder Editor, *The Print* and Former Editor-in-Chief, *The Indian Express*

This is an amazing true story of a life of incredibly varied experience—a 'must read' for all.

Tarun Das, Mentor, CII

Generous in his praise and scathing in his criticism, Swarup gives us revealing insights into the complex world of Indian administration. Laced with interesting anecdotes, this book gives an account of the challenges he faced in his career—the Babri Masjid period, the RSBY scheme, coal block auctions, and the mess that permeates India's education system. That India continues to progress against all odds is due to officers like Swarup, who stick to their principles, withstand enormous pulls and pressures and are able to deliver while remaining within the system.

Dr Ambrish Mithal, Padma Bhushan, Renowned Endocrinologist

The book authored by Anil Swarup is a must read for the new entrants to the civil services as he has given a new definition to the ethos and spirit of bureaucracy.

Anil belongs to that rare breed of civil servants who have the spine and are willing to take on the powers that be, both in the bureaucracy as well as the political class, who consider governance, not for promotion of public good, but for private gain. Anil, in his book, has shown that a civil servant can go beyond rules and regulations and become a motivator, a leader of men and an innovator in formulation of policies. He stood for what he thought was right and earned the reputation of being straightforward, telling his bosses, where he thought, they were going wrong, and, not worrying about the consequences.

After reading his book, one feels that the governance of the country is in safe hands, so long as we have civil servants like Anil Swarup.

Yogendra Narain, Former Chief Secretary, Uttar Pradesh and Former Secretary General, Lok Sabha

I have known Anil since our days in the Mussoorie Academy. A standout from the beginning and winner of the Best Officer Trainee award, he has always been frank and forthright in his views. His book traces the remarkable career he has had in UP and the Government of India, giving the reader an intimate view of some absorbing episodes of national importance. A page turner.

Parmeshwaran Iyer, Secretary, Rural Sanitation (Swachh Bharat), Government of India

अविरल

समय रुका नहीं, हम क्यूँ ठहर गए?
अभी तो हम चले ही नहीं, फिर क्यों थक गए?

उठो पथिक मत भ्रमित हो, धूमिल अंधियारों में।
श्रेष्ठ वही जो घिरा नहीं हो, क्षणिक निराशा में।

जागो, जगाओ, मन मत बहलाओ।
एक मसीहा, तुम भी बन जाओ।

Preface

What a journey it was in the Indian Administrative Service! I do not know whether it could have been more fulfilling. My life was full of challenges and that was the beauty of it. There was so much to be done, so much that one could do and so much excitement! I spent sleepless nights in the sheer excitement of the potential. The excitement was there from the first to the last day of my service. This book is an attempt to share some of my experiences in serving the poorest of the poor and the richest of the rich. I was blessed to have come across some outstanding officers and individuals who inspired me to remain committed and on track because they had delivered.

Mr Yogendra Narain, the unflappable performer, was one of the many civil servants who inspired me not only to perform but also to keep penning down my experiences. This book is an outcome of what he had instilled in me a couple of decades ago.

Mr Prabhat Kumar, efficiency and candour incarnate, who rose on to become the Cabinet Secretary, was the one who goaded me to organise my thoughts and articulate them in the form of a book. I never worked with Mr D K Mittal, but he was my role model as he epitomised clarity of thought and decisiveness. Ajay Bhalla who later became Union Power Secretary was instrumental in laying the foundation for clearing the coal mess that forms a substantial part of this book. Vivek Bhardwaj, the then Joint Secretary in the Ministry of Coal who was responsible for carrying out the coal block auctions (though I walked away with most of the credit), helped me construct the chapters on coal. Anita Karwal and Santosh Mathew were a couple of outstanding officers in the Ministry of Human Resource

Development who contributed substantially in structuring and articulating my thoughts on the chapters related to Education.

Contribution of Vijay Kumar Juneja, my Private Secretary, was enormous in all the backstage work from typing, re-typing, re-re-typing the manuscript over and over again, and keeping track of everything.

Behind every successful officer, there is a sacrificing family. I am not sure whether my tenure as an IAS officer was successful or not, but my family did make a lot of sacrifice. Initially, it was my parents and my siblings, who sacrificed their comfort to ensure that I got the best of education in an expensive public school, then my wife, Ruchi; daughter, Aditi and son, Apurv equally led a spartan and disciplined life to ensure that we lived within our means. My wife was also a sounding board for the thoughts expressed in the book. There could not have been a better critic.

Author

Foreword

When I moved to Delhi in July 2009, with the responsibility of setting up the Unique Identification Authority of India (UIDAI), I was a 'newbie' to the Government. The then UPA Government was gracious enough to appoint me as Cabinet Minister. In the first few weeks, I had realised that just having a rank did not get you very far in navigating the byzantine corridors of power in India's capital. I had clearly bitten off a lot, having set myself the task of giving over a billion Indian residents a unique identity number. I tried to make up for my ignorance of the arcane ways that the system worked, by meeting everyone and anyone who could give me some insights. While conversing with my writer and intellectual friend Gurcharan Das, I heard about the Rashtriya Swasthya Bima Yojana (RSBY) project and of course, about the leader of it— IAS officer Mr Anil Swarup. I was intrigued and decided to meet Anil.

Anil had his office in an unexpected place, the dusty Jaisalmer House, one of the many royal residences that dot New Delhi. Within an hour of meeting him, I realised that I was in the company of a very unusual bureaucrat. He was very passionate about his project, to implement health insurance in India at a national scale. Anil was the first to implement smartcards for such a huge project. He had cobbled together a motley coalition of supporters, from the World Bank to the German development agency, GTZ. He was spearheading a 'health' project, being in Labour & Employment, not in the Ministry of Health.

Being a bureaucrat in the Indian Government and aspiring to reach the top, the best strategy is not to take risks, not to take decisions, be circumspect in voicing opinions and seek safe jobs in established ministries. Anil did not follow this guidebook. Controlling the turmoil of UP in the initial years as an officer in the Coal Ministry to his stint as Secretary, School Education in the Central Government, Anil has beautifully juggled passion, risk, challenges and quick decisions to make a difference and leave a mark. He has been ever willing to do 'start-ups' like the RSBY and the Project Management Group (PMG). Moreover, his visualisation of the impact of technology in bringing development and transparency has helped him to bring in many innovations, from biometric authentication in the RSBY to the on-line portal in the Project Management Group to e-auctions in coal.

Over the last few years, decision making in the Indian Government has become crippled, thanks to the overhang of the 5Cs (CBI, CVC, CAG, CIC and Courts). Anil has been open and forthright on how this has hampered Governance. To speak about this, while still in service, was indeed brave.

It is to Anil's credit that even in a subsequent reincarnation he would like to be an IAS officer! His candid and engaging book is a must read for those who want to understand the complexities of Indian administration and how a few good men and women can make all the difference.

Nandan Nilekani
Chairman Infosys and Founding Chairman UIDAI (Aadhaar)

Contents

Early Years

My future was perhaps decided the day I was born. My father did it for me. He himself had fulfilled his father's dream of becoming an engineer and now, in turn, he wanted his son to join the 'elite' Indian Administrative Service (IAS) observing the respect and recognition accorded to the IAS officers. My schooling had to be planned accordingly. As he was a government employee with a job that entailed frequent transfers, he decided to place me in a hostel. After a few unsuccessful efforts, I finally got admission at the renowned Sherwood School in Nainital. However, homesickness got the better of me and I came back home. Another attempt was made. This time, it was the famous Colvin Taluqdars' College in Lucknow. I did my best to run away from there as well. But my mother put her foot down and I had to stay put. She could be extremely persuasive and firm when she felt that a course of action was good for me. She had done most of her education after her marriage. Hence, she understood the importance of quality education.

Before joining Colvin, I had not won a single award, despite desperately wanting to. In those difficult days, it was my father's discipline and mother's persistent encouragement that kept me going. They did not allow me to give up. I was conscious of the fact that I had to succeed not only for myself but also for them. Self-motivation enabled me to emerge as an all-rounder.

My next destination in education was also pre-determined. My father was not only meticulous in planning, but also quite good at execution. I was then to join the Muir (Amarnath Jha) Hostel, Allahabad University. It was considered a breeding ground for civil servants. My accomplishments in extracurricular activities ensured a spot in the hostel. In academics, I switched over from Science to Arts. After having slogged hard in Class XII, I now had sufficient time to focus on language and personality development. My articulation, verbal and written, was poor. As I made conscious efforts to improve, I faced ridicule by my peers. However, I was focussed and carried on.

I wished to be an accomplished debater. It was at Allahabad University that I forayed into debating. The drill was to pen down the details and commit them to memory. On one such occasion, as I walked to the podium, I got so nervous that I forgot what I had learnt and got tongue-tied midway through the delivery. Finally, I had to walk off the stage.

I also claimed to be a good singer. The occasion was the annual cultural festival at IIT, Kanpur and I was participating in a solo vocal competition. That day as I started singing, I realised that I had picked up the wrong note. The discerning audience discovered the dissonance before I did. I was booed out. I was shattered. On the following day, there was a debate competition and I was representing Amarnath Jha Hostel, Allahabad University. I was mentally not prepared to face the audience. One of my seniors, Sanjay Srivastava (who later did very well as an IAS officer) asked me to forget the past and to focus on the debate. This pep talk made a huge difference. When my name was announced the following day, the audience started chanting— 'the singer'! However, the debater in me persisted, and I went on to win the first prize. After that, there was no looking back.

The Kothari Commission Report provided a new dimension to the entrance exam for Civil Services. In the absence of any precedence, the preparation for the exam was an exhaustive one. I had read a lot and learnt a lot. This resulted in my undoing during the first attempt. I found it difficult to package the answers within the alloted duration. I could not make it to the IAS but qualified for the Indian Police Service (IPS), an achievement that didn't quite enthral my father. He was crestfallen. He had never thought that I would ever fail him. But I was determined to make amends. The focus during the second attempt was to pin down the answers within the stipulated time. This made all the difference. I made it to the IAS in the second attempt.

Police Academy: Hectic days and sleepless nights

Having qualified for the IPS, I had joined the National Police Academy at Hyderabad before taking another shot at the IAS. The National Police Academy provided training to officers that had qualified for the IPS. The schedule was hectic. We used to start our day early in the morning with a run within the campus and strenuous physical exercises which were then followed by drills and classes that ended late in the afternoon.

Amidst the rough schedule at the Police Academy, the probationers did find time to fraternize. Once a colleague approached me with a problem that many of us used to face— "I am unable to sleep at night". "Why can't you sleep?" I asked. His answer surprised me, "The price of petroleum is at peak. It is a huge problem for the country. I am restless". I was a bit perplexed. I asked, "Can you do anything about it?" "No. What can I do? But I am really concerned as it will lead to inflation". I said, "If you can't do anything about it then there is no point spending sleepless nights over it". He agreed and looked pacified for the moment. I thought it was all over. But, I was wrong. After a couple of months, he approached me again, "I am still unable to sleep at nights". "Why now? The petroleum prices seem to have stabilised," I asked.

"Petroleum prices are not the present issue," he retorted. "Then what is bothering you now?" I tried to probe further.

I found his response quite amusing, "India's growth in population is a grave concern". I agreed with him. However, I reasoned that by spending sleepless nights in future, he would only add to the population problem. He perhaps got the hint and never approached me thereafter.

Our training at the Police Academy was made worse by an over-enthusiastic Assistant Director of Out-door Training (ADOT). We preferred calling him an IDIOT. We, as a group, revolted against being treated as guinea pigs and in an unusual manner. In a marathon race to select a Course Adjutant, all of us ensured that the bulkiest amongst us came first.

I had to leave the Academy midway the training as I qualified for the IAS. This must have come as a relief to the Director as I was becoming increasingly inconvenient. I was sad to leave behind a fabulous group of officers. I cherish till date the memorable moments I had with them.

National Academy of administration: Living in paradise

It could not have been better. After the grind at the Police Academy, it was like living in paradise in the Queen of Hills, Mussoorie that houses the Lal Bahadur Shastri National Academy of Administration. It was the right ambience to train the budding civil servants. Post-independence, the IAS replaced the Indian Civil Service that was constituted by the British to rule India. Prior to 1959, the IAS officers were trained at Metcalfe House in Delhi. In 1959, the two-year training was shifted to Mussoorie. In addition to the training, it provided an opportunity for everyone to be in close proximity with other officer trainees, from all parts of the country, who were selected on merit to serve the country. This association proved handy right through the careers. The focus, quite aptly, therefore, was on knowing each other during the foundation course that also involved a trek to the mountains and a visit to a village. These were a few of our numerous unforgettable experiences. However, what marred this ethereal experience was an unsavoury episode of a probationer misbehaving with a lady colleague. This left an indelible scar. After the Foundation Course, those belonging to services other than the IAS departed. We missed these friends in the first phase of the training when the atmosphere turned a trifle sombre.

Skits, mimicking staff members, were the highlights of our stay at the Academy. Everyone looked forward to those skits that were short, crisp, and hilarious. The staff had a tremendous sense of humour and never took it amiss. One cannot forget the drawl of Mr Sundar Burra, so inimitably mimicked by Naresh Prasad ('Nainoo' as we called him), the cultivated accent of Mr Ravi Mohan Sethi and the stance and gait of Mr Alok Sinha, the then Deputy Directors who were mimicked to perfection on stage. The clenched teeth diction of Mr S C Vaish, the then Joint Director, too was rather remarkable and made for enjoyable skits.

Bharat Darshan too gave moments to savour. The officers were split into five groups and were taken around the country to get a first-hand look at it from the perspective of a budding administrator. The excursion included an attachment with a tribal village for few days as well as to an army unit in the border areas. One got to know more about their colleagues. There was an enthusiastic runner who used to run in the morning, no matter what the conditions were. And, when it rained, he spot-ran in the washroom. He was also known to use up an enormous amount of talcum powder. A few of them were always on the lookout for a liquor shop. However, we discovered the most interesting bit when we strayed into the red-light area on one of the beaches in Goa in the middle of the night. We had reached Mormugao at an unearthly hour with no place to stay. It was an amusing sight as most of the budding bureaucrats looked visibly embarrassed but a couple of them were thrilled at having hit the 'treasure'.

As they say, it takes all types to make this world … it was true of the bureaucrats as well.

A game of cards: Changed the game for me

Following the British tradition even today, Collectors/District Magistrates head District Administration. During the British era, their primary job was to collect revenue and maintain law and order. However, post-independence and with the passage of time, their role has undergone a change, and the focus has shifted to developmental work. They are also supposed to be mentors to the probationers. My first boss was indeed a mentor but, as was often the case in Uttar Pradesh (it is much worse now), he did not stay for long and a new one arrived. As was the practice, I went over to call on him at his 'camp' office (a euphemism for office at home). The new incumbent preferred to run the show from his residence. Despite having informed his staff (read 'steno babu') in advance, I was made to wait. I waited for a couple of hours in sweltering heat along with a number of visitors awaiting *darshan* in the waiting room. As there was still no message from him, I decided to leave. The Collector did not care. Neither did I. My training continued unabated despite my inability to show my face to him. That was the beauty of the system. He did not bother me as I did not fit in his scheme of things, and I did not bother him either. It took a different attribute to get noticed.

It was New Year's Eve and a get-together was organised at the officers' club. Having spent a few months in the district, I had made a few friends. We got down to playing cards and soon were joined by the Collector. As the clock struck 12, we wished each other and carried on with the cards. I went on to win the game and cost my boss INR 300 (in those days it was one-fourth of my monthly salary). It was in the early hours of the morning that we quit and headed home to get some sleep. At around 1130 hours, there was a knock at my door. On opening the door, I was presented with an envelope sent by the Collector. In it, I saw an order appointing me as Sub-Divisional Magistrate. This was quite unusual as I was still a probationer (Ironically, the same Collector refused to appoint my batchmate as Sub-Divisional Magistrate when he completed his training as he had turned down the offer to marry the daughter of the Collector's boss, the Commissioner of the Division). Perhaps, the recognition had come on account of my accomplishment in the game of cards.

Discovering the truth

A case related to an overloaded passenger vehicle is fresh in my memory. I had been just posted then at Kasia (Kushinagar), a subdivision of Deoria district in the eastern part of Uttar Pradesh (UP) bordering Bihar and was not conversant with the way business used to run there. That vehicle was carrying 21 passengers, much beyond the permissible limit.

Executive Magistrates also used to try cases for violation of traffic rules in those days. On that day, the courtroom was crowded as there were several cases lined up for consideration. I did not believe him when the prosecutor told me about the overcrowded taxi. As per my understanding, a passenger vehicle could under no circumstances accommodate 21 passengers. I summarily discharged the case as another instance of high handedness on the part of the enforcement agency.

As the days went by, I gradually got acquainted with the region. Another day, while travelling to the sub-division, I noticed an overcrowded vehicle coming from the other side. Out of curiosity, I stopped that and asked the passengers to disembark. It was an amusing scene. They kept pouring out. They were standing precariously on every possible protrusion or projection of the vehicle. A few of them were seated on either side of the driver. The count ended at 23. This was two more than the vehicle I had discharged a few days ago.

I realised that anything can happen in this part of the country.

Management Skills of a Different Kind

What they don't teach at business school

It was 1990. I was posted as the District Magistrate (DM) of Lakhimpur-Kheri. A bank branch located at a mofussil town was looted by some armed Sikh terrorists. I immediately rushed to the location. The then Superintendent of Police, Dr Harish Chandra Singh, who gave me this message, was already on the way. This daring police officer was subsequently awarded for handling the situation proficiently. Lakhimpur-Kheri had been infamous for terrorist strikes, but for me, it was baptism by fire. I had taken over only a few months earlier and was not truly clear about my role in such a situation. In fact, when the terrorists (five of them) were gunned down after an eighteen-hour-long encounter, I realised that I had not fired a single shot. It was not required at the moment; the primary task was to control the enthusiastic public which in an attempt to support the police was eager to take a direct part in the operation. This zeal of the locals to support the administration prevented any further strikes in the district.

I continued to be in the hit list of the terrorists but that was a professional hazard and a lifetime experience. The presence of the DM had not only boosted the morale of the police force, but had lent legitimacy to the encounter (in the adjoining Pilibhit district, the police force was soon to be hauled up for a false encounter). The well-built, 6-feet-plus men despite being armed with AK-56 rifles succumbed to a determined assault by the men in uniform and the courage of the people around. Traditional skill was of no use in such a battle-like situation.

The 1990 *Ram Janam Bhoomi* issue appeared as a test for all those who were in charge of districts. There was communal tension all around, with more than half of the districts under curfew. Lakhimpur-Kheri took pride in keeping the tension under check without imposing curfew. This was achieved at a considerable cost. The officers were on their toes round the clock for days together. One had to spend several nights in *kotwali*. This was a war of attrition and one had to ensure that the administration was always on the move. Handling a situation that had the potential to destroy public peace required skills which were never mentioned in the management courses of Business School. It was an assessment of one's endurance and the capacity to keep the morale high even when the chips were down.

The management and control of Mandal aftermath that preceded *Ram Janam Bhoomi* upsurge called for different skills altogether. The administration had to deal with motivated yet immature minds of youths that were besieged with a sense of deprivation. This was again when the administration was asked to manage the chaos which was an outcome of the games that some people chose to play. On several occasions, one's oratorical skills were put to use while convincing the youth that beyond Mandal there was a future. This argument did not cut much ice to begin with, but one had very few options at one's command.

Most of the time then was spent in managing manufactured crises. It was a lesson in crisis management. My colleagues in the district subsequently confirmed that the situation had only become worse over the years. With governments changing every two years (or even less), the average tenure of a DM had come down to less than a year. Activities centred both on managing the politicians and handling the crisis created by them. Those that have perfected the art of managing the politicians have had longer tenures. However, all said and done, despite the erosion in the institution of the DM, it still commands a lot of authority and one's conventional managerial skills are not really put to test. Well-established systems have lasted for almost a century. Thus, a lot many activities take place irrespective of the character and capabilities of the DM. They can still afford to be the 'brown sahib' in certain respects, provided they have mastered the art of allotting requisite time to the people who matter. Being assisted by an army of officers, be it revenue, development or law & order functions, they can always bank upon the competence of some of their subordinates without indulging in challenging work themselves. Now that tenures are extremely short, they can get away with it as well. However, committed DMs can do a lot, if they so desire, by motivating those under them in the redressal of grievances, in fostering development and in toning up the revenue machinery. Despite the status quoist nature of the job, an initiative on the part of the DMs is normally received and accepted quite well.

Yes, Chief Minister

The election of the Etawah Assembly segment had been countermanded by the Election Commission during the 1991 Assembly Elections in UP. However, Bharatiya Janata Party (BJP) having obtained majority had formed the Government under the leadership of Mr Kalyan Singh. I was appointed as Director, Information (DI) despite not having known or met Mr Kalyan Singh in the past. Later on, I discovered how sensitive that post was.

It was an early morning informal chat at the residence of the Chief Minister (CM). The Chief Secretary and the Director General of Police were also present. The CM was agitated by the large number of rallies (seven in all) to be addressed by him on a single day for Etawah by-election. He asked his personal staff to put him in contact with the DM so that the last two rallies could be cancelled. Though I was new to the assignment and his political rallies were none of my business, I offered some unsolicited advice. I told him that it would not be appropriate to cancel the rallies at the last moment. With my recent experience as a DM, I also told him that a lot of preparatory work goes into rallies and there would be a lot of anticipation on the ground. The CM, apparently, did not like my intervention, at least in the beginning. He retorted, "How do you expect me to address so many rallies in a day?" The Chief Secretary nodded his head vigorously in approval with the CM and his plight. He kept nudging me to keep quiet. However, I carried on undeterred. I politely replied to the CM that my suggestion was my professional view, and; it was up to him to take the final call. There was pindrop silence for around half a minute (to me it appeared much more than that) during the course of which the Chief Secretary kept nudging me. The CM finally broke the silence. *"Anilji, aap theek keh rahe hain".* (Anil, you are right.) He agreed that it would not be appropriate to cancel the scheduled rallies. The Chief Secretary agreed with him immediately again, and to my relief, the nudging stopped forthwith.

Udyog Bandhu: Task of a facilitator

During the British era, the office of the DM was held in awe and respected greatly. Post-independence, this was whittled substantially but the respect was still there. He was still the head of District Administration and the formal representative of the Government at the district level. Contrary to this, the office of Executive Director, Udyog Bandhu was not so authoritative. Udyog Bandhu was set up to promote industrialisation in the state of UP. As against an uncertain tenure and almost an unquestioned authority, I was catapulted into Udyog Bandhu in 1995 where the tenure was secure but there was hardly any authority to go with it. I was now supposed to interact with the suave and ostensibly benign industrialists. The language of communication was different, the audience much more sophisticated. No longer was I to assuage the wounds of a particular section of the society or to ensure that the writ of the administration was run through the length or breadth of the district. In fact, my role underwent a metamorphosis. It was now that of a facilitator. Whereas in my position as a DM it was the government machinery which was instrumental in solving the problems of an average person, I was now attempting to remove the bottlenecks created because of government functioning to clear the path for industrialisation. I was no more the deliverer of goods, issuing orders and ensuring their compliance. My task was now that of an intermediary between the industrialist and various departments of the government. The assistance in this task was not provided by hard-boiled bureaucrats but by professionals. What came handy was the experience to appreciate and analyse problems. There was no longer the queue of servile *mulaquatis* awaiting *darshan* for small favours as was a common sight in the district.

Unlike my stint as a DM, the boundaries in the new assignment were not defined. There were few opportunities in the district to go beyond one's remit. However, one's preoccupation with law & order hardly spared time for any such creative activities. It was not so in the new dispensation which not only provided time but adequate professional assistance and scope to indulge in creativity. Thus, attempts were made, both in and outside the country, to project UP as a destination for investment. My ability to analyse and articulate the potential of industrialisation in the state was given a shape. The transformation was not an easy one as the attributes required to work as a DM and those as a facilitator were different. A facilitator had to go out and meet people and convince them about the good things in a state. The only similarity (and an extremely comforting thought) in both the roles, of the DM and of the Executive Director, was the conviction that a lot could still be done both with the politician and with the bureaucracy. The dead end was still far off. The clear stream of reason had still 'not lost its way in the dreary desert sand of dead habit'.

The PICUP story: Pulling up a sinking ship

'*It is an amazing story about leadership, about professionalism, about vision and strategy and more than anything else, it is about hope that it generates for the future of UP'*, wrote *the Times of India* on 24 April 2005 while appreciating the turnaround of an organisation which was in the red for the past nine successive years. The turnaround had come about in just ten eventful months.

I received a message on 15 June 2004 that the Chief Secretary had called me urgently. Little did I imagine that I was about to be sent to one of the most challenging assignments of my entire career—to an organisation which boasted of being one of the best in the country but had fallen from grace and had been headless for the past two months for the first time in its history, as there were no takers. An apologetic Appointment Secretary tried to explain why I was being 'dumped'. However, it did not really matter to me as government orders were supposed to be carried out in right earnest. Thus, began a difficult and challenging but an extremely enjoyable journey at PICUP.

The Pradeshiya Investment Corporation of Uttar Pradesh (PICUP) was set up in the 1970s to finance small and medium industries in the state. It did extremely well during the first couple of decades but like many other financial institutions started incurring losses.

I took over as the Managing Director (MD) of PICUP almost immediately after receiving the order. As I walked into one of the most impressive buildings in Lucknow, I found the atmosphere inside sepulchral. Not only was the organisation in bad shape, but the atmosphere also conveyed despair. The initial discussions with the officers only confirmed my apprehensions. The issue was not whether but when the organisation would die its natural death. The Chief Accounts Officer broke down as he narrated how the creditors (in all 541) of the company were harassing him as the company had an accumulated liability of more than INR 900 crores. The losses had accumulated to more than INR 500 crores and the net worth had been eroded to an extent of INR 365 crores. Officers were deserting PICUP like rats desert a sinking ship.

What followed were sleepless nights spent pondering over the manner in which this organisation could be brought out of the mess that it had gotten into. There was no immediate remedy in sight. The initial analysis of various financial statements also threw no light on how this organisation could survive. A turnaround was unthinkable.

It happened at midnight after a week of sleepless nights and the idea came out of the blue. Why was the organisation writing off all interest when it could recover some of it? Why was it liquidating its assets only to pay interest and not the principal debt? In answers to these questions lay the remedy for this ailing organisation which appeared to be terminally ill. A rough presentation was drafted before dawn and as the sun rose in the east, so rose the fortunes of PICUP.

The presentation was discussed with senior officers of the organisation and the formula appeared to be extremely simple: 'Stop paying the interest and use the money to liquidate the principal liability'. The top officials bought this idea immediately and the first hurdle was crossed. A formal presentation was prepared before the Board. Though there were not very many other options available, the Board reluctantly agreed. Most of the directors believed that it would not work as the creditors would not agree to waive the interest on bonds which were guaranteed by the government. Moreover, the liquidity required to liquidate these bonds was not available. However, the landmark resolution was adopted after an extremely persuasive presentation.

A crack team for carrying out the resolution of the Board was constituted, and informal messages were circulated to as many creditors as possible saying that PICUP, which had defaulted in the payment of interest was now willing to offer a one-time settlement to the creditors. After initial reluctance, came the first offer and that set the ball rolling for others to follow. These offers were circulated to other creditors. Simultaneously, the financial ill health of the corporation was publicised as a part of a well-defined strategy.

On another front, all-out efforts were made to liquidate some shares in the market to generate liquidity for liquidating the liabilities. More than INR 100 crores were raised during the year for this purpose. Favourable market helped the cause. The Almighty was certainly helping those who were helping themselves.

Communication channels, formal and informal, were put in place to convey a variety of messages. Appeals were addressed directly to the employees and they were made to understand what was being planned for the organisation. Sacrifices were made at the top and those below induced into making such sacrifices. With the Managing Director himself travelling much below his entitlement, it became easy to secure a similar commitment from others without any formal order. Apart from saving precious funds, it brought the whole organisation together in the task of rebuilding. Several other steps were taken to reduce expenditure. Thus, officers were encouraged to use e-mail in place of telephone, no new vehicle was sanctioned, security arrangements were re-organised to cut cost and the guest houses entailing huge costs were closed down to cut expenses. Efforts were also made to bring about transparency through the implementation of paper and file tracking system. This also speeded up the decision-making process.

As there was a severe financial crunch, non-financial motivational tools were utilised to seek the involvement of the officers. Recognising good work and public acknowledgement of successful efforts and initiatives and visible support to such initiatives went a long way in motivating a demoralised workforce. Involving each level in the decision-making process facilitated the easy acceptance and ownership of each decision. Consequently, there was a lot more commitment to the implementation of these decisions. Officers were given the opportunity to gain the trust of the management without prejudice. Trust begets trust. This is precisely what happened in PICUP. Officers started making personal sacrifices for achieving organisational goals. A new work culture evolved.

The organisation grew in confidence as more and more creditors approached for settlement of dues, voluntarily waiving all the interest that was due. As the fiscal year drew to a close, an incredible 223 creditors had offered to settle their dues worth more than INR 100 crores. This resulted in a saving of more than INR 34 crores. After a gap of nine years, PICUP declared a profit in excess of INR 40 crores. There was hope and a spring in the step of the employees who started believing that they can and, hence, they could. This self-belief was infectious as the organisation started reinventing and reorienting itself.

With the liquidation of principal liability, the consequent reduction in the interest liability and the likelihood of this trend to continue, the organisation earned a profit in the following years as well. This confidence enabled PICUP to look beyond its traditional role of lending which in any case was stalled because of the poor financial health of the organisation. Recognising the good work done by PICUP in the recovery of its dues, several nationalised banks appointed PICUP as their agent for recovery of their dues. This was likely to generate substantial income in the corporation in the years to follow as PICUP had the core competence to undertake such activities.

PICUP was now on the threshold of becoming a premier consultancy organisation. With several Engineering & MBA graduates, the potential had always been there. It was only waiting to be exploited. Consequent to the setting up of Consultancy Division, a number of consultancy projects came to PICUP and many more were in the pipeline. These ranged from consultancy on asset management to IT applications in Uttar Pradesh State Industrial Development Corporation (UPSIDC).

The Phoenix had begun to rise from the ashes.

Two wrongs do not make a right

A number of heavyweights had pulled PICUP down. But here was a really big man, a leading journalist in a leading daily. The company that he had set up grew bigger as another leading journalist, who had worked in various dailies and was known to move in high places, got involved. This company incurred heavy losses and to make up for these losses, they came up with an ingenious idea of setting up another venture with a substantial contribution, by way of equity, from a state-run financial corporation PICUP. The loss made by the existing company was the equity contribution of these leading journalists in the new venture. With the blessings of few politicians and top bureaucrats, the new venture came into existence. The first wrong was committed at the cost of public money. These two journalists, the promoters of this new venture, were supposed to keep the finance corporation posted about the activities. However, the promoters found themselves too big to condescend to supply any information about how the public money was utilised. Even the share certificates, a mandatory requirement, were not given to the corporation. No one raised a finger against these big men even as the financial corporation hurtled down an irretrievable precipice because of a willful default of such companies which it had financed.

Surprises never cease to happen. The finance corporation started turning around as the officers started chasing the defaulters. Notices also got issued to these journalists. It was an affront to them. No one so far had ever dared to question them. For them squandering public money was as much their right as it was of politicians or select bureaucrats. I faced tremendous pressure. However, I was busy rebuilding the Corporation brick by brick. I was in no mood to wilt or relent. The efforts were bearing fruit and the prospects of the organisation were looking up. Impressed with the improvement, ironically the leading daily, to which one of the journalists belonged, published an article commending the progress. It called the revival 'an amazing story about leadership; about professionalism; about vision and strategy… '. It did not really matter to these journalists, the senior bureaucracy or the top politician whether the corporation was turning around or not. What really mattered to them was the fact that journalists who mattered, or could matter, were being pushed to do the right thing. This right was wrong for these select bureaucrats and politicians as they had their own definition of right and wrong. When I refused to toe the line, I was eased out. A pliable bureaucrat was brought in my place to wrong the right. No more notices were issued to the powerful journalists. In fact, a proposal was pushed in the board meeting to write off the amount which was contributed by the state financial corporation by way of equity. The second wrong had been committed and it was much worse than the first one.

Some bureaucrats and a few politicians had benefited through some 'supportive' reporting during the period when these journalists were attempting to settle their case. Once the 'settlement' was through, all hell broke loose. The leading daily screamed through a headliner on the front page that the Chief Minister had amassed property worth crores. The journalist who had been one of the beneficiaries in the 'settlement' filed the report. To the officers of the financial corporation, it was poetic justice as they had suffered because of the indiscretions of the powers. For the journalist, it was an attempt to reestablish his credentials. But for the top politician, it was a sacrilege, a *vishwasghat.* All efforts were then made to reopen the case and to nail the journalist.

On 'board' with the bats and rats

The transfer order was expected, and in fact, desired. It came because of the stand I took against oral directions from the CM's office to suspend officers working in the department headed by me. They sought to scapegoat the officers and grab the headlines. I refused to be a party to this charade and requested a transfer. Hence, when the orders came, I was not surprised.

There were, however, surprises galore when I arrived in Allahabad to take over as Member (Judicial), Board of Revenue. The first one occurred as I was driven to the Board office from the railway station in a car, in which, except the horn, everything else made a noise. The driver of the car kept vanishing intermittently. The car was still moving. I could not contain my curiosity and peeped in front when he performed the vanishing trick the next time. The gear of the car was partly broken, and the driver had to bend down every time to change the gear. This partly explains why the posting as Member, Board of Revenue was considered a punishment.

The condition of the board office was no better. It was the 21st century for the rest of the world, but the board was still struggling to come out of the 19th. The building, however, was majestic, befitting the majesty of the Raj in its glorious days. The first floor was occupied by more bats than human beings. Some portion of the roof carried the colour of the bats! The noise made by them competed with the rattling sound of the manual typewriters which had otherwise been banished from most of the government offices.

The room of the Member-in-charge was huge in all dimensions. That perhaps was the only impressive part in an otherwise grossly unimpressive existence. The carpet (if you could call it one) was partly consumed by the rats. There was a small office table fit to be kept in a cubicle and a few rickety chairs, apart from an unstable sofa whose tapestry had worn off. There were wires all over the place, but the only lamp kept on the office table didn't work (perhaps unable to decide which wire to pick electricity from!).

The task of the Members was to hear appeals and revisions against the orders of the lower courts in revenue cases. However, it soon became evident that except the clients, no one seemed to be interested in the disposal of cases. Barring some laudable exceptions, the senior officers bided their time and awaited a better posting. The concern of not-so-senior Members was to keep the quota going. The bar too was interested only in getting dates. As the presiding officers were indifferent, the demoralised staff obviously lacked any initiative. The board epitomised inefficiency and indifference. The bats and the rats ruled the roost and the case files languished and gathered dust. The whole atmosphere was depressing. For me, it was one of the greatest challenges of my career.

To begin with, I was clueless. I had no formal control over the other members who were partly responsible for the mess. The officials were an ageing lot. Most of them were 'hard boiled eggs' with little scope for change. My own Personal Assistant (PA) who was due to retire shortly had never seen a computer. Hence, the justifiable expression of shock and apprehension on his face when requested to attempt typing on a newly stalled computer would always be fresh in my memory. It is a different story that he soon started using computer efficiently and took pride in it. He set an example for others in the office. This happened in just four months.

Being familiar with IT tools that I had used to solve several problems in my previous assignments, I knew that those could be handy there as well. The primary issue was motivating the staff. The officials were laid-back, inefficient, indifferent, and as dishonest as they could be in the given set of circumstances. They obviously resisted any sort of change. At the outset, the objective was clearly defined. I was convinced that justice delayed was justice denied. Hence, the precise objective was to speed up disposal of cases and to bring about transparency in the process of disposal. A dialogue was initiated with the local representatives of National Informatics Centre (NIC) to prepare a proposal for the hardware required and to work on the software. Past association with this organisation came handy and it was more than willing to assist. The proposal was prepared and sent to the headquarters for approval. The Chairperson provided unconditional support and that made a lot of difference. In the meanwhile, the software for the functioning of the courts was prepared.

Then began the most difficult task. A number of interactive sessions were held with the officials in small groups to sell them the idea of improving the state of affairs and the utility of IT applications. Gradual inroads were made. They were then put through a familiarisation process on the computers which were borrowed from districts through personal influence and with the Chairperson's help. The sanctioned hardware was installed much later. Problems, both personal and official, of the officials, were attended to. They were encouraged to contribute through suggestions in the decision-making process. Officials who did well were recognised and appreciated publicly. Gradually they came to accept and own the changes that were being brought about in the organisation. Quite a few of them even took pride in what they were now doing, coming to work on time and keeping their desk clean. Soon this 'disease' spread. After initial resistance, there was a healthy competition amongst the divisional clerks in terms of updating records through computers. This meant that the Cause List could now be generated automatically for any given date on a real-time basis. The ground was, therefore, prepared to host it on the website to make it freely available to anyone. It also enabled the presiding officers to closely monitor the disposal of cases.

Even as an attempt was being made to banish the ghost of opacity and inefficiency, the worn-out carpet was removed, the record room programme outlined, and file movement streamlined. The bats which epitomised this culture were literally banished, and a plan was chalked out for taking care of the rats as well. The disposal of cases too improved drastically. The result was visible, but the challenge now was to prevent these 'bats' from returning in future. On enquiry about the status of the bats, few years down the line, I was informed that for some unknown reason the bats had chosen not to return.

When It All Came Crashing Down : 6 December 1992

The Babri Masjid had been a bone of contention between two communities for decades. It all began during the 19th century though the structure was apparently built in the period 1520-29 CE by Mir Baqi on the orders of the Mughal Emperor, Babar. The mosque was located on a hill known as Ramkot. Many Hindus believed that Baqi had destroyed a pre-existing temple of Lord Rama at the site. They also believed that Lord Rama was born there. This belief emanates from the documents of Maharaja Sawai Jai Singh—a Rajput noble in the Mughal Court. In the Kapad-Dwar collection in the City Palace Museum of Jaipur, there is a sketch map of the Babri Masjid site. The map portrays an open courtyard and a structure resembling Babri Masjid with three domes. The courtyard is mentioned as *Janmasthan* and shows a *Rama Chabutara* (a raised platform named after Lord Rama). In 1853, a group of Hindu ascetics occupied the site and claimed ownership over the structure. In 1855, after a Hindu-Muslim clash, a boundary wall was constructed to avoid further dispute. Subsequently, Muslims offered prayers in the inner courtyard and Hindus on the raised platform.

The dispute acquired a legal dimension when in 1877, Syed Mohammad Asghar, the guardian of the structure, filed a petition with the Commissioner of Faizabad requesting for restraint on Hindus who had raised a *chabutara* on the spot regarded as the birthplace of Lord Rama.

In December 1949, the Akhil Bhartiya Ramayan Mahasabha organised a nine-days recital of *Ramacharitmanas* just outside the mosque. On the morning of 23 December, the event organisers announced that the idols of Lord Rama and Sita had appeared miraculously and exhorted Hindus to come for darshan. Given the sensitivity of the issue, the government then declared the mosque disputed area and locked the gates. The gates were unlocked decades later in the year 1986 when Hindus were given access to the site.

A massive campaign was subsequently launched to build a Ram Mandir on the site. It was in these set of circumstances that the BJP under the leadership of Mr Kalyan Singh came to power in Uttar Pradesh and I was appointed as Director, Information and Public Relations.

Mr Kalyan Singh took his job in right earnest. Immediately on assuming office, he made his intentions clear to provide honest and purposeful governance. He was keen to convey that he meant business. A list of honest officers was sought to run critical posts like DM and Secretaries of Departments. Certain social evils, like mass copying in school examinations were sought to be reined in. The cabinet meetings would go on for hours, discussing policies on various issues before taking a final call. The construction of the Lord Rama Mandir, the issue on which the BJP rode to power, was always a hot topic of discussion but Kalyan Singh's focus lay in converting Uttar Pradesh into an *Uttam* Pradesh. With a set of bright officers in his Secretariat, like Sanjay Aggarwal and Anant Kumar Singh (both of whom rose to become Secretaries to Government of India), he left no stone unturned to achieve that objective. Improvements were clearly in evidence in the form of delivery of services at the field level and in the posting of competent officers. These officers were provided security of tenure (the state was otherwise infamous for a flourishing 'transfer industry') and necessary backing to implement policies. The bureaucracy was performing. However, what happened on 6 December 1992 changed everything.

It was a Sunday. It should have been a holiday. However, with thousands of *karsevaks* (volunteers for construction of the temple in Ayodhya) from all over the country congregating in the town of Ayodhya (the birthplace of Lord Rama), there was tension simmering on this cold Sunday morning. A similar event had taken place in July but had concluded peacefully. This was what Mr Kalyan Singh hoped would happen once again. Ironically, he himself, through his initiatives had provided a ray of hope to the state that had fallen into despair.

In my capacity as Director, Information and Public Relations, it was my duty every morning to brief him about the media coverage. On this day, there was an uneasy lull with a storm brewing in the east. Hence, I arrived at his residence at 4A Kalidas Marg, a little earlier than usual. Mr Kalyan Singh, usually a paragon of composure and confidence, looked perturbed, sitting all alone in a room where he received guests. He was speaking to someone over the telephone as I walked into the room. Even though the previous congregations at Ayodhya concluded without any mishap, he was opposed to such congregations. He was focussed on setting things in order in the state and was being recognised for what he was attempting. Within a year of his government, he had left a mark.

Even his critics admired his honest and no-nonsense approach to resolving issues. He did want a grand temple at Ayodhya and was diligently working towards a peaceful and amicable consensus. He was totally against aggressive posturing that was the hallmark of right-wing religious organisations.

This was a time when mobile phones did not exist, at least in India. Apart from Doordarshan, there was no other live channel. Teleprinters and landline telephones were the primary modes of communication. In absence of a 'live' telecast, it was difficult to gauge the ground reality. Kalyan Singh was getting intermittent updates from Ayodhya. He even had a word with Lal Krishna Advani who was in Ayodhya then. Everything seemed to be under control. Or, so it appeared. Then came the news—some of the *karsevaks* had broken the cordon and climbed the domes of the old structure. The structure had collapsed. Kalyan Singh was crestfallen and livid. Along with the Babri structure, his dreams of re-building UP had come crashing down. His subsequent telephonic conversation with Bhairon Singh Shekhawat (the then Chief Minister of Rajasthan) reflected his angst against the party leadership. He reiterated that he was against such a congregation, but his objections were over-ruled and no one listened to him. As a final comment, he stated that he would take responsibility for what had happened and resign forthwith. He then asked me to get a paper and wrote a brief resignation letter to the Governor (I later learnt that a formal type-written resignation letter was indeed sent). In this letter, he took responsibility for what had happened without providing any explanation. He clearly mentioned that no one else should be held responsible. It is difficult to believe now but there used to be politicians who had the courage to take responsibility. No sooner had he completed penning down his resignation than he regained his composure. Just then the Principal Secretary, Home, entered the room. As I accosted him to the Chief Minister, he whispered into my ears *marwa diya* (finished us). How true it was in the context of the effort that was being made to resurrect the state. It had all come crashing down. UP never recovered after this crash.

Serving the Poorest of the Poor

Health Insurance

Healthcare in India was financed through various sources—individual out-of-pocket payments, central and state government tax revenues, external aid and profits of private companies etc. National Health Accounts data of 2004-05 showed that central, state and local governments together accounted for only about 20% the total health expenditure in India. More than 78% of the health expenditure comprised un-pooled, out-of-pocket expenditures, one of the highest in the world. External aid to the health sector accounted for negligible 2% of the total health expenditure.

The Government of India recognised inequities in its healthcare delivery and financing infrastructure and introduced various measures to overcome it. One of these measures was to increase the budgetary allocations for healthcare. The Government target was to increase its spending on healthcare from the 1.1% of GDP to 3% of GDP. However, just an increase in the budget for healthcare was not a solution in itself. There were limitations in the absorptive capacity of the public healthcare system, apart from the manner in which these funds were utilised.

Successive governments in India had introduced various financing mechanisms to provide financial security to vulnerable segments of the society in the previous few years; for example, in 2003, the central government had launched Universal Health Insurance Scheme (UHIS). Similar state level health insurance schemes were launched by the states of Punjab, Kerala and Assam. However, most of these central or state government funded schemes ran into problems due to the poor design of the policies, lack of clear accountability at the state level, lack of sustained efforts in implementation, weak monitoring and evaluation, unclear roles and responsibilities of different stakeholders, and lack of awareness among the beneficiaries.

For people living below poverty line (BPL), an illness not only represented a permanent threat to their income earning capacity, in many cases it resulted in the family falling into a debt trap. When they needed the treatment, the poor often ignored it because of lack of resources, fearing wage loss, or until it was too late. Even if they did decide to get the required healthcare, it consumed their savings, forced them to sell their assets and property or cut other important spendings like children's education. Alternatively, they had to rely on huge debts.

The central government felt the need to introduce a national-level health insurance scheme for the vulnerable sections of the society. Learning from the experiences of other major government and non-government health insurance schemes in India, it was decided to launch a health insurance scheme that later came to be known as the Rashtriya Swasthya Bima Yojana (RSBY). The BPL population was considered as the first target of this scheme. Later on, many categories of unorganised workers like construction workers, domestic helps, street vendors were added to the scheme as well.

How it all began

'You are in Labour'—came the cryptic message from one of my colleagues who was concerned enough to find out where I would be posted after the mandatory 'cooling' in the 'hot' state of UP.

This was a surprise to me. More surprises were in store as I walked into the Office of Directorate General, Labour Welfare in Jaisalmer House. The dust-ridden carpets in the rooms made me wonder why they were there in the first place! The files and piles of papers were in harmony with the surroundings. It was an unsuitable environment for any kind of delivery. I was soon to discover that in the Ministry of Labour & Employment, nothing was delivered. Quite aptly, the moment you 'would deliver', you would be out of labour. This gradually became clear to me after a number of meaningless and time-consuming meetings and many much-touted tripartite discussions where often confusion was only compounded. There was no attempt to find solutions or to arrive at any agreement. Each stakeholder used to say what he had to say. There were long-winding statements and discussions, acrimonious on occasions, but merely to reiterate the stated position. No one was prepared to yield an inch. Consequently, no one gained any ground. All these sessions were perceived as zero-sum game where any one's gain could only come at the cost of the other party. As a result, everyone was a loser. However, these rituals were observed religiously, especially at the annual national conference. It was a recurring demand to stretch it for a few more days. As it was too hot in India in the month of June, there was an annual visit to Geneva to find solutions to labour-related issues. As every participant benefitted personally in these jaunts, no one ever questioned the need for such visits. Even the periodic cost-cutting measures announced by the Government did not affect these 'important' tours. The problems remained where they were. The department continued to be in labour without delivering anything. It failed to address labour-related issues in the right spirit.

The Central Trade Union had also done precious little. It was frustrating. The focus, almost always, was on the miniscule organised labour force and informal workers that had no social security cover were left high and dry. These 430 million unorganised workers were languishing. Occasionally huge noises were heard. There was a demand to deliver everything when even a little appeared unlikely. No one had any idea about how to implement all these grandiose designs. Everyone believed that if only money were made available, the problem could be solved. Those manifestly representing the cause of unorganised workers had neither any representation nor any clue about their plight. This facade had continued for more than five decades. However, the Government finally made a move, and providing health insurance was the first step in that direction.

Dr Manmohan Singh, the then Prime Minister, was concerned about the plight of the workers. Despite his 'liberal' credentials, he was concerned about the *aam aadmi*. His was a sincere desire to push the 'inclusive' growth agenda. He was perhaps conscious of the fact that 'social welfare spending not only reduces inequities and uncertainties within a rich society but also bolsters the confidence and trust within the society to be more generous'. (*Common Wealth* by Jeffrey D Sachs)

Despite a common belief to the contrary, he was perhaps aware that 'if a society cannot help the many that are poor, it cannot save the few that are rich'. (John F Kennedy)

He was keen that the workers of the unorganised sector should be provided with a health insurance cover. However, no one had a clue about how to do this. The earlier efforts of providing health insurance by the government, including the much-publicised UHIS, had proven to be non-starters. The health insurance component under the National Rural Health Mission (NRHM) had very few takers. Experience elsewhere in the world also did not offer any solution. Moreover, Labour should have been the last department to visualise, conceptualise, articulate, and roll out a health insurance scheme. But, since there were no takers, Ministry of Labour was asked to do this job.

Seeds of the RSBY sown

We gathered at the International Labour Organisation (ILO) country office in Delhi to discuss the annual approach. The weather was pleasant in the month of February. However, the tenor of discussion was the same as any other government meeting. The speeches were mechanically delivered, presentations made, and a general roadmap laid out. Ironically, there was neither discussion on the roads travelled the previous year nor evaluation of the distance travelled. No one seemed too keen to find concrete deliverables. The discussions were about to come to a close without any new ideas or new conclusions. It seemed to be a waste of time, except for the time spent in bidding farewell to a bright officer of the ILO who had completed her tenure in India and was now moving to another country.

Just when the meeting was about to conclude, a suggestion was floated to set up a task force to examine various aspects of implementing health insurance in the country for the poor. This task force would include experts from the World Bank, ILO and the related ministries. This suggestion came out of the blue and one could discern scepticism around the table. However, what perhaps clinched the issue was the fact that the Prime Minister himself had hinted that immediate thought should be given to health insurance. In any case, there was no harm in setting up such a task force, little did we know that this was to lay the foundation for one of the most farsighted schemes. This scheme came to be known as the RSBY.

The idea was great but the trick was how to make it happen. "No matter how good any idea is, it has no value unless other people understand it, embrace it as their own and help you implement it". (*The Writing on the Wall* by N R Narayan Murthy)

And, this was a real challenge.

Faulty database

BPL database or the lack of it was exasperating. It was indeed a miracle that many schemes were riding on a database which was non-existent, erroneous, incomplete and, on occasions, incomprehensible.

There were two sets of issues. One was data related and the other one technology related. On the data front, the situation was appalling in some states. The worst-case scenario was the incomplete data. This meant a fresh survey, which was a time-consuming exercise. In a number of states, the data did exist, but it was not digitised. The implication was that this data had to be entered in the computer system, and for this purpose, teams had to be set up. Then there was the next stage, where the data did exist in the digital format but not in the desired format. Reformatting required technical capability and all states did not have this capability. These capabilities had to be developed. Considering the time and effort required, a number of officers just gave up. The states had never looked at the BPL data in such details as was required of them under the RSBY. There were several issues relating to the data size, census codes, data presentation (alpha, numeric or a combination of two), the primary relationship and the like. If anything slowed the process of roll out, this was it. The RSBY could not have taken a call on the veracity of the BPL data. It was assumed that the state was correct though this was not always true. A conscious decision was taken that verification of data could not be taken up under the RSBY. This did create a few problems in the field while rolling out smart cards, but it was not practically possible to make verification a part of the roll out of the RSBY. However, internal inconsistencies were taken care of through validation software that was prepared by the World Bank. Attempts were also made to collect written representations from those that were left out of the list. The insurance companies were not authorised to make any corrections on the spot. Their mandate was to roll out the cards based on validated data downloaded from the website.

Evolving a conceptual framework and standards

There were many experts, both national and international, and they appeared to know everything about health insurance. But, perhaps, not as much about the Indian context—its diverse process, iniquitous economy and a complex society. The task force set up to evolve a policy frame could only analyse the ongoing health insurance schemes. This analysis failed to provide the conceptual understanding of a workable health insurance scheme in the Indian context at the national level.

Fortunately, at least during the initial stages, no one was questioning the efficacy of insurance as an instrument for delivery of health care. Perhaps no one gave the RSBY a serious consideration. However, once the scheme was initiated, all hell broke loose. The 'supply-side' proponents began to condemn the 'demand-side' approach adopted by the RSBY.

There were myriads of unanswered questions, ranging from the rudimentary to more sophisticated ones in the context of insurance. Should there be a single framework for the entire country or, given the diversity of the country, should the states be allowed their own framework? The concern with allowing the states to have their own platform was if there were diverse frameworks, how would the interoperability issues be addressed? Given the migratory nature of the beneficiaries, portability of benefits and interoperability could not be compromised. The duration of the insurance had to be decided. Should it be for one full year or till the end of fiscal year? Should it be for a fixed period? If yes, then what should be this fixed period? Should this period be determined for each district separately or should the state be taken as the unit?

There was a huge debate relating to outpatient department (OPD). The policy almost came unstuck on this issue as there were strong feelings both in favour and against. The potential moral hazard ultimately clinched the issue against OPD cover in the beginning. The inclusion or not of pre-existing diseases was debated at length. Excluding pre-existing diseases was not found to be practically feasible. Maternity benefits had to be initially excluded at the behest of the Ministry of Finance. It was ironical that the Ministry of Finance would take a call on health-related issues. We were not even pennywise to be pound-foolish. Wisdom finally dawned and subsequently, maternity benefit was allowed to be included.

Contribution by the beneficiaries, especially considering their impoverished status, was a matter of debate as well. Quite surprisingly, there was a greater opposition from the bureaucracy. What finally won the argument was the ownership issue. It was suggested that the benefit would be valued more by the beneficiaries if some token amount was taken as registration fee annually. It would also help evaluate the scheme later. The scheme was finally proving that if the 'product' was good, even the poor were prepared to pay for it.

The next issue in question was the definition of 'family' and how many members would get the benefit. The definition had to be changed midway to enable inclusion of parents though the number of beneficiaries was limited to five. The sisters-in-law and brothers-in-law were, however, kept out as were some relatives. It was difficult to affirm whether it was a right decision to restrict the benefits to only five members when the family size is much larger in several areas. Then, if the family was larger than five, how would the decision regarding exclusion be finalised?

There was an ideological debate as well. Should both public and private insurance companies be allowed to compete? The UHIS was restricted to public sector insurance companies. This restriction was one of the reasons why the scheme was a non-starter. Therefore, both public and private sector insurance companies were allowed to bid in order to promote competition under the RSBY. The beneficiary could avail the benefits at any of the network hospitals, both public and private. The role of insurance companies was also a moot point. Should there be one insurance company for each state or should district be taken as a unit? Should multiple insurance companies be allowed to operate in each district to provide a choice to the beneficiary? Would it be practical to do so? Can the beneficiary make such a choice? Settlement of insurance claims had to be considered upfront to sustain the business interest of the hospitals.

Question arose—could there be an electronic settlement of insurance claims as they were vast in numbers? What data was needed by the insurance companies to settle these claims?

Could it be digitised? With a view to ensuring paperless transactions under the scheme, the decision was to go in for electronic settlement of claims. There were still issues relating to the software, its maintenance and cost. The insurance companies were obviously allowed to have access to the hard copies in the hospital for random verification.

At a conceptual level it had to be decided whether there should be criteria for empanelling the hospitals. To begin with, a liberal criterion was adopted. There were indeed complaints about empanelment of hospitals that were grossly ill-equipped and had pathetic sanitary conditions and could hardly be called hospitals. However, there were more puzzling questions related to medical and surgical procedures. Another concern was whether the costs of surgery or other medical procedures should be uniform for the country.

The conceptual framework of the scheme could also not overlook sustainability. Any scheme is not worth the effort if it is not sustained over a period. Most of the government schemes adopt the 'intensive monitoring model' of sustenance. Thus, everything is monitored periodically at each level of hierarchy with the lower rung burdened by the presence of the 'monitors'. The RSBY sought to address the issue differently. It was perhaps the first ever effort to evolve a 'business model' for a social sector scheme.

Standardisation of procedures and processes was found essential to ensure interoperability right through the country and also to obviate unnecessary duplication in evolving such procedures and processes. Thus, documents such as tender, contract, MoU between the centre and the states were standardised, as were medical procedures and the costs thereof. It was a complex exercise involving several contentious issues. This was in the backdrop of World Bank's inability to produce an acceptable tender and contract document for the state of Karnataka. Determining such rates for medical procedures which could be acceptable to the hospitals across the country was also quite a challenge. For a mass scheme where health services are to be bought for large population, the indicative rates fixed were almost 30-40% lower than the prevalent market rates. The rates prescribed were not mandatory and the states were allowed to change them though there were to be uniform rates within the state. However, almost all the states adopted the rates suggested by the central government. Quite interestingly, the hospitals too accepted these rates even though these were well below their usual charges, perhaps this was because now they could fully utilise their bed capacities.

There were ideas and suggestions galore during the exercise of standardisation. None of these ideas were tested but such ideas could not be wished away. Each argument had to be settled to the satisfaction of the decision makers.

The standardisation in terms of IT applications was even more complex because even in private health insurance not many IT systems were being used at that time and paper-based identification and claim process was the norm. Technology was the key in the rollout of the RSBY. The breakthrough came when Rishi Gupta and his team from Financial Inclusion Network and Operations Paytech Limited (FINO) brought before me a Point of Sale (POS) machine to demonstrate that biometric data could be captured through a mobile gadget. Now it had to be decided which aspects could be standardised by the central government and which of those could be left to the states. Then, a right balance had to be struck between flexibility to the states and non-negotiable mandatory aspects. Standardisation itself had to be of a nature which could be marketed to the states.

The initial reaction

Health insurance had not happened anywhere in the world on such a large scale. Initially, almost every single factor worked against the situation. The terrain in which such a scheme was to traverse was inhospitable. The instruments provided to make it work were inappropriate, inadequate and blunted by indifference and inertia. Ironically, someone within the bureaucracy wanted to walk away with the credit even before it happened. This person had accomplished that in climbing up the bureaucratic ladder in the past and succeeded. However, not many had a clue about how it would happen. Yet it happened.

The scheme itself was not a miracle. But, in India, it probably was! At the end of the first year, the scheme was 'seen as a model of good design and implementation with important lessons for other programmes in India' and an 'interest in the RSBY programme was expressed in a number of other countries' (World Bank). The *Business Outlook* magazine rightly dubbed the concept of smart card of the scheme as one of the 25 ideas that would change the world. Gurcharan Das in his weekly column in the *The Times of India* called it 'the best Diwali present' and *The Wall Street Journal* quoted one of the beneficiaries describing the scheme as 'the best scheme India has'. It is a moot point whether the scheme deserves the acclaim that it got, but it is true that the scheme got going despite all odds.

The RSBY was truly unique. Unlike many other government schemes, the RSBY evolved as a product catering to the requirement of the target group. The characteristics and requirements of the BPL families were analysed and the conceptual framework was built on these analyses.

The prospective beneficiaries (the consumers) were, by definition, poor. The consumers could not be expected to raise resource upfront to seek medical assistance and then make a claim. They were, largely, illiterate and in no position to undertake documentation to settle claims. Many prospective beneficiaries were migrants, primarily in search of employment. Hence, there was a need to allow them to avail of the benefits in the destination states. Migrant workers of Bihar, East UP, Odisha and the like could claim benefit under the scheme at any network hospital of the state where they had migrated. Through the smart card, these problems were taken care of. The RSBY also enabled splitting of smart cards so that the migrating head of the family could 'carry' some of the health cover credit with him and leave the rest for his family. The amount to be split was at the discretion of the beneficiary.

The RSBY, in fact, empowered the consumer, the BPL family, by giving them a choice. Under the existing hospital service, a BPL member could not afford a private hospital. Under the RSBY, the beneficiary had a choice to select from any of the networked hospitals, both in the private and public domain, anywhere in the country. They were not tied down to a delivery point as in the case of almost all the public sponsored social welfare scheme. The National Rural Employment Guarantee Scheme (NREGS) tied them down to a project and the Public Distribution System (PDS) to a shop. The beneficiaries under these schemes had no choice. But the RSBY beneficiaries had a choice; they could decide the delivery point and this was their empowerment. This was the first ever effort made in this regard. None of the insurance schemes operational in the country had such portability across such a wide network of hospitals. This was a record.

A large number of other health insurance packages, both in the public and private domains, did not cover pre-existing diseases but the RSBY did. It helped to avoid inconvenience to the consumer in deciding which disease was pre-existing and which was not. Considering the numbers involved under the RSBY, it would have been practically impossible to determine pre-existing diseases and there would have been innumerable disputes. Though, the inclusion of pre-existing diseases had an impact on the premium, it made it much simpler to implement.

The scheme aimed at being cashless to cater to the peculiar characteristics of the target group. The only cash transaction was in terms of transport expenditure of INR 100 to be provided by the hospital to the beneficiary when he got admitted. The package rates covered all the aspects—medicines, food, lodging etc., and the payment of the package rate was made by the insurance company to the hospital.

The only payment (INR 30) that the beneficiaries had to make was at the time of issue of the smart card. This also marked the first ever attempt to seek some contribution from the BPL family for delivery of benefits. As the card was not free, the beneficiary 'valued' the card and demanded services as they had paid (even though a small sum) for it.

The scheme aimed at paperless operations. No documentation was needed for issuing the smart card or even at the time of admission or discharge from the hospital. Most of the surgical procedures were standardised, codified and costs frozen. The claims of the hospitals were also largely settled electronically as the requisite information in prescribed format was flown through an electronic gateway. This was unique and unprecedented, as much imperative, in the context of the paperwork that would have otherwise been generated in a scheme of this scale.

The RSBY prided itself in being a business model which sustained the scheme. There was an inbuilt financial incentive for the public and private players to do what they ought to do. The insurance companies had an incentive to issue as many smart cards as possible because the payment to them was a multiple of the number of cards issued by them. Similarly, the hospitals were not chasing away the beneficiaries because they got compensated for the treatment given to the beneficiaries. It was indeed a win-win situation for all the players, including the respective governments because if the insurance companies and the hospitals did what they ought to do, the objective of the RSBY got fulfilled.

It was also a rare initiative in that it was an attempt to evolve a social sector scheme through public-private partnership. Initially, the funding for the premium came from the government, but the scheme allowed both the public and private players in the field of insurance and health services to play a critical role in implementation of the RSBY. However, consequent to the successful roll-out of the scheme, the private sector and non-governmental organisations expressed willingness to fund the premium with a view to utilising the smart card platform for providing health insurance cover to their constituents. The public and private institutions worked in tandem to make this scheme a success.

Ever since the IT revolution in the country, such tools had been used in the public domain as well. However, perhaps it was for the first time that

IT tools were being used on such a large-scale and in the rural parts. The IT applications also made this scheme one of the most foolproof ever. An elaborate Key Management System (KMS) developed under the able guidance of S K Sinha, an officer from the National Informatics Centre (NIC) which supplemented the biometric operations ruled out any possibility of duplication or misuse.

The RSBY did not call for creation of a separate bureaucratic framework to implement the scheme. Quite interestingly, despite its large-scale and complex backend, no additional post was created at the central level during the first two years. Even at the state level, by and large, the existing bureaucratic structures were utilised to implement the scheme. This, however, threw up innumerous challenges in terms of reworking the priorities at various levels, reorientation and sensitising of the decision makers and training of the field-level functionaries.

All in all, the scheme was different. It was different in the context of its conceptual framework. It was different in the way it was actually rolled out. And it was different in the manner in which it impacted the lives of the poorest of the poor in this country.

International agencies: The RSBY owes a lot

The idea of a health insurance was first raised in a discussion at the country office of the ILO. Marc Socquet represented the ILO in the task force. He took part in a series of discussions and helped the group to analyse the ongoing health insurance schemes in the country. He was instrumental in giving some especially useful inputs in terms of compiling and evaluating the ongoing health insurance schemes within the country. However, quite inexplicably, the contribution ceased thereafter. There was a sudden discernible indifference towards taking the concept to its logical conclusion. Mere preparation of a document seemed to be the objective of this organisation.

There was lukewarm response to overt and covert overtures to enlist the support of the ILO in testing the waters. They did not extend the contract with Marc Socquet. However, along with the United Nations Development Programme (UNDP), later on, the ILO went on to recognise the scheme as one of the top social security schemes in the world. The scheme details were published in a document brought out jointly by these agencies. The ILO subsequently got associated with the scheme by way of a couple of experimental projects to test the feasibility of using the RSBY smart card platform for outdoor patients as well.

Barak Obama has rightly said in his autobiography, *Audacity of Hope* that "the World Bank has a reputation for funding large, expensive projects that benefit high priced consultants and well-connected local elites but do little for ordinary citizens—although it's these ordinary citizens who are left holding the bag when the loans become due. Indeed, countries that have successfully developed under the current international system have at times ignored Washington's rigid economic prescriptions by protecting nascent industries and engaging in aggressive industrial policies. The IMF and the World Bank need to recognise that there is no single, cookie-cutter formula for each and every country's development".

Those who helped the RSBY happen

The RSBY was fortunate to find a set of experts from the World Bank who did not belong to the category that Obama had in mind. The RSBY, in fact, would not have happened without active support from the World Bank, more specifically from Robert Palacios and his team that comprised Philip O'Keef, Changquing Sun, Sumita Chopra and later Wyly T Wade. The proactive interventions of Robert ensured that the interface with the World Bank was seamless. His pleasing demeanour and never-say-die spirit stood the scheme in good stead. He would always be on the lookout for solutions and would often find one. He managed to find some funds from somewhere (he had to explain his conduct later to his principals back in Washington) to put in place the first enrolment software. The software demonstrated that the smart card technology could work. The Labour and Employment Ministry did not have the wherewithal to administer such a technology-driven scheme. Palacios ensured that all possible technical assistance was made available. Unfortunately, the World Bank had its own share of 'not-Palacios' who give a bad name to this institution that can do wonders. Obama perhaps referred to such persons that represent the opaque, inflexible, inaccessible and insensitive part of the World Bank. Even with the agreements in place, the ministry got entangled in the bureaucratic red tape that threatened the scheme, but Palacios ensured that the tenure of the consultants was extended.

Changquing was rechristened 'Chain (Relief) Singh' because he brought some relief. Notwithstanding the frustrating circumstances, he used to find solutions to complex data management issues. Despite numerous visa-related problems which forced him to leave the country intermittently, he remained dedicated to the implementation of the scheme. His perseverance and commitment to tasks were exemplary.

Sumita Chopra was incomparable. Engaged as a consultant by the World Bank to help in the implementation of the scheme, she ate, drank and slept the RSBY. She probably knew more about the scheme than anyone else associated with the scheme. Her technical knowledge was as much an asset as her approach. She was, therefore, required to be almost everywhere. She travelled to all the state-level workshops and made lucid powerpoint presentations. She even featured in the first documentary film on the RSBY and put up a professional performance. She became an epitome of the RSBY.

The assistance provided by Philip O' Keef in standardising various documents, which were so crucial in the context of an implementation of the scheme, was priceless. A number of previous such ventures had failed because such standardisation had not been undertaken. The scheme lost his services midway as he had to leave the country because of some personal reasons, but the scheme shall always be indebted to him for the contribution he made when many people did not believe that the scheme would see the light of day.

Wyly T Wade was different and added a new dimension to the group. His understanding of technical aspects and ability to fathom the nuances of ticklish and complex issues came handy. He was alert, almost always, despite an apparent laid-back demeanour.

Dr Nishant Jain of Deutsche Gesellschaft für Internationale Zusammenarbeit GIZ was a bundle of energy. The Ministry of Labour did not have an agreement with GIZ (and for some strangely inexplicable reasons did not want one initially) but the organisation found value in the scheme and used funds from the ongoing arrangement with the Ministry of Health to assist the RSBY. Much of the success of the scheme after its launch can be attributed to the small team of GIZ that became an intrinsic part of RSBY movement. The most remarkable feature of this association was the total compatibility in terms of objectives and approach that was spearheaded by Dr Nishant Jain. His professionalism and concern for details came handy. None of us could believe it when he showed up a couple of days before his wedding at a state-level workshop and volunteered to make a presentation. As the RSBY spread far and wide in the country, he was the one who kept the momentum going, shuttling from one state capital to the other, trying to find solutions to operational problems.

Chopra was sharp and technically sound. The scheme, given its scale, did run into many technical problems. Some such problems had to be attended overnight and on various occasions, she not only found solutions to the technical problems but also volunteered to pay for pizzas and coffee. She believed in meditation and never lost her cool even in the most trying of circumstances. It took a tremendous effort from everyone for the scheme to be implemented. The RSBY happened and continues to happen because of such individuals.

An institutional arrangement was finalised with GIZ during the fourth year of the scheme. With it, arrived Rolf Shmachtenberg, the team leader of the GIZ team. Rolf was tall in every sense, contributing immensely to all the discussions. To prove the efficacy of the smart card, he got the RSBY team to implement a couple of smart card projects in two municipal corporations in a technologically advanced Germany and his sense of humour never deserted him. The GIZ was now formally involved, in helping to meet several emerging challenges as the scheme expanded to other categories of workers.

Support from international organisations like the UNDP and the UNICEF was useful in addressing several issues that beset the rollout of the scheme. At the central government level, it was easier to get certain tasks done by these agencies as compared to the effort involved in getting clearances from the Internal Finance Division whose performance was perhaps determined by the number of objections they raised.

Funds from the Department for International Development (DFID) came in handy in addressing an important aspect of the scheme. Reaching out effectively to the beneficiaries was a challenge that the scheme faced. It was in this context the Poorest Area Civil Society (PACS), funded by the DFID, played a key role. Rajiv Khosla, the country head of PACS and several field functionaries contributed substantially in meeting this challenge.

Indeed, the scheme would not have happened without the support that came from international agencies. These agencies and individuals were conscious of the fact that the details of each aspect of the scheme were to be worked out 'at the ground level, in the villages and cities themselves rather than in the capitals or in Washington'. (*The End of Poverty* by Jeffrey D Sachs)

Ministry of Labour was itself a challenge

The Ministry of Labour that got the mammoth task of evolving and implementing the scheme was grossly ill-equipped to handle this complex scheme of unprecedented proportions. What made the task even more difficult was a lack of appreciation of the complexity of the scheme. It was treated like any other scheme of the government. The focus was on form, rather than substance. Commitments were made for various launches without any consideration to the nuances. Perhaps, N R Narayan Murthy had these bureaucrats in mind when he commented, "Our bureaucrats have to learn to stand up for their beliefs and values rather than be subdued by their respect for their superiors—political or otherwise".

During the first year of implementation of the scheme, it was much worse. The only concern of the person at the helm of affairs was to somehow please the powers that be. Hence, a directive was issued on 12 September 2007 which stated that the issuing of the smart cards under the scheme ought to begin from the 2 October. The Mahatma would have never approved of such a farce. Before issuing such a directive, no attempt made to find whether necessary prerequisites were in place for such a launch. The idea, perhaps, was to show off that it could be done without realising that it could undo the entire scheme. Such attempts at roadshows had come a cropper in the past. There was such an example in the ministry itself when the smart cards were launched in the presence of the then President of the country, but nothing happened thereafter. However, it was a directive and was demanded that it ought to be carried out. Fortunately, this was resisted much to the displeasure of the authorities, and the scheme was saved from being consigned to the same fate as some of the other public-sponsored smart card projects.

There were 'experts' within the Labour Ministry who tried to fiddle with the conceptual framework without fathoming the consequences of what was being 'pushed'. Thus, the inclusion of outdoor patient care became a major cause of disagreement. Such an inclusion and the inherent 'moral hazards' would have derailed the entire scheme. Not only were the suggestions unsound, the experts sought to steamroll the changes through. Notwithstanding potential personal penalization, the team resisted coercion and did not compromise with the rollout of the scheme.

The inability to recognise the fact that the RSBY was different and, hence, required a different treatment, was creating all the problems. Considering the complexity of the scheme, it had to be marketed not 'pushed', it had to be facilitated not monitored and it had to be understood, not skimmed through. The scheme needed a lot of patience and commitments and attributes that are alien to many bureaucrats. Fortunately, there was indeed a small number of officers who believed in the scheme and in themselves too. They were prepared to take risks, innovate, experiment, learn and evolve. The group never gave up despite an indifferent, unsupportive and, on occasions, a hostile environment which was beset with distrust, pettiness, insecurity and obstinacy. The marketing of the scheme entailed a lot of travelling but one was never sure whether the tour programme would be approved during the initial years of the scheme. It depended upon the whims and mood of the top boss. This uncertainty caused embarrassment on a number of occasions. Viewing the initial success of the scheme, the World Bank had sent in an invitation for an officer to make a presentation and to discuss the scheme with the representatives of other countries at the annual conference in Washington. After due approval, necessary commitments for the visit were made. However, without assigning any reason, the concerned officer was forced to curtail the visit from three to one day. More time was spent on travelling than in Washington. It reflected the pettiness with which issues were handled.

A lot of time was wasted in pursuing files relating to the scheme as there were timelines to be adhered to. The central government had agreed to set up independent societies in the states to impart flexibility of the operations. However, it was dragging its feet for a similar arrangement at the centre. All efforts to build institutions to ensure sustainability of the scheme were stonewalled. In the name of building institutions what was now being constructed was a hierarchy of bureaucratic and political committees. Such structures had failed to deliver in the past but only a few bureaucrats could rise above the desert sand of dead habit.

Yet, the RSBY happened. It happened despite an ill-equipped ministry which was the biggest bottleneck in the roll-out. The scheme could be executed because it was seen as a unique opportunity to visualise, conceptualise, articulate, implement and evaluate an idea by a small set of bureaucrats within that very ministry. It could be executed because this small group took decisions even at the cost of risking their careers. This was certainly not an easy task. Officers like A V Singh and Urmila Goswami who constituted the core group never gave up or gave in to any pressure which was not in the long-term interest of the scheme. Singh was extremely fond of poetry and came up with an appropriate couplet or an anecdote to diffuse any tense situation. Goswami was fully conversant with all the financial procedures. She also knew how to use these procedures to fast track files.

Big names behind the RSBY

The unqualified support and guidance from the Additional Secretary (later Special Secretary), S Krishnan, during the formative years, and the Secretary, Prabhat Chaturvedi, in the later years went a long way in making this scheme a success. The scheme went through challenging times when it was in its evolutionary phase. There was indeed pressure from anybody who was somebody to deliver everything yesterday. It was during these times that the poise, patience and perseverance of Mr Krishnan made all the difference. He sat through meetings for hours as Chairman of IT Committee as various issues relating to IT applications were thrashed out. He encouraged open discussions and never misconstrued any statement or opinion. The whole team stayed motivated by his positivity. Prabhat Chaturvedi belonged to a different ilk of bureaucrats. The scheme saw an exponential growth during his tenure.

The exponential growth came to a grinding halt with the retirement of Prabhat Chaturvedi. The new secretary who took over was a well-intentioned bureaucrat but had serious doubts about the efficacy of insurance as an instrument to deliver healthcare. All the expansion plans were put on hold as the RSBY team once again came under pressure within the ministry. The scheme was being lauded elsewhere but the fundamentals were being questioned at home. There were departments that were willing to implement the RSBY for providing insurance cover to their constituents, but the Ministry of Labour became possessive and reluctant to permit them. A national platform was now reduced to a departmental one. The momentum of the scheme suffered. As the scheme ran out of funds, the Ministry of Finance was requested to provide additional allocations. However, in a letter to the Labour Minister, the Finance Minister pointed out that since outlay for the Ministry of Labour had increased, the allocation for the RSBY could be provided from the savings from other schemes of the ministry where the funds had been underutilised The Ministry of Labour was insistent that the funds allocated to other schemes would be utilised. The paucity of funds almost derailed the RSBY as premium could not be paid to the insurance companies who in turn delayed settlement of the claims of the hospitals. There were a large number of cases where the beneficiaries were not provided assistance in the hospitals as huge claims were pending. The Ministry of Finance finally relented and allocated money for the scheme from contingency. Because of callous indifference within the Ministry of Labour, the scheme had to go through unnecessary trouble when funds could have been easily appropriated from the other schemes in the ministry itself. The funds for the other schemes remained underutilised.

The prospects changed once again when the new secretary became the biggest supporter of the scheme. This transformation came over a period of time as he gradually understood the nuances and purpose of the scheme.

Involvement of other central ministries:
A game of trust and mistrust

It was indeed ironical that those ministries that had been largely unable to roll out health insurance package in the past attempted to determine the course of the RSBY as well. Almost all the government schemes take a long time to roll out because there is an attempt to plug all possible loopholes, apprehending misuse and abuse. The entire system is beset with mistrust. There is paranoia. Hence, nothing moves. The RSBY was different. However, it was an uphill task to make the central ministries believe that.

The Finance Ministry still believed that without its stranglehold on each file dealing with funds, all hell would break loose and the system would eventually collapse. Hence, the Finance Ministry insisted on processing every premium payment related file through the internal finance division. With 600 odd districts in the country and the monthly release of premium based on the number of smart cards issued every month, there would be around 7200 files going up and down the bureaucratic ladder without any value addition. The scheme had evolved differently in all other contexts except this one. The world around was changing but the Finance Ministry lived in its own world. It still continues to do so.

A department of the Ministry of Finance had earlier been assigned the responsibility of implementing the UHIS. The scheme was a virtual non-starter. Now, the department had an opportunity to participate in the rollout of the RSBY. They did so initially, but then parted ways as they perceived conflict of interest because public sector insurance companies had also participated in the bidding process. Because of this, the work of Ministry of Civil Aviation and the Ministry of Petroleum would come to a halt as several decisions that they take would affect such companies as these are owned by the government. However, this department was unrelenting. In any case, not many in the government had a clue about how to overrule the diktats of the Ministry of Finance.

The Health Ministry was at a loss. They had ventured in the field of health insurance as a part of NRHM, but nothing had happened in the first year. As against this, the RSBY was rolling in the first few months of implementation. The Central Health Ministry was nonetheless cooperative in extending all possible aid by way of enabling the use of *Rogi Kalyan Samitis* at the district level to take part in the RSBY. It was, however, quite intriguing that the Health Ministry did not take a view about continuing with the health insurance component of NRHM. They even toyed with the idea of an insurance component in the proposed National Urban Health Mission. Ironically, the target group under the RSBY and these missions were the same. Fortunately, the idea was shelved although it happened after a lot of time was wasted in various meetings.

Some bureaucrats in the Ministry of Information Technology raised more non-technical issues than technical ones when the scheme was discussed with them. Their logic was simple. As the proposed scheme and the technology had not worked in the past, they would not work in the future. It was surprising that innovation was being resisted by those who should have championed it. The RSBY had to evolve independent of this ministry. The IT revolution in the country had taken a similar path and the rest, as they say, is history.

The Ministry of Rural Development would not part with the BPL data which was critical to the success of the scheme. Quite interestingly, the ministry did not have the necessary data in the desired format or in the format prescribed by the ministry itself. The formats had been designed by the Central Ministry long ago, but the states had not quite conformed to it. However, once the RSBY was set into motion, it generated curiosity about how the back-end data management under this scheme would help in data management of MGNREGA, another flagship scheme of the country.

The decision of the government to extend the RSBY to such Mahatma Gandhi National Rural Employment Gurantee Act (MGNREGA) beneficiaries who had worked for 15 days or more during the previous fiscal year did create a potential synergy between the two flagship schemes of the country.

The officers of the Planning Commission were extremely cooperative. Even the presence of hostility at some levels did not make much of a difference.

A presentation before Montek Singh Ahluwalia, Deputy Chairman served our purpose. He was quite impressed with the concept and the initial progress under the scheme. His enquiry, whether a presentation was made before the Prime Minister, did the trick. The other members, as well as the bureaucracy in the Planning Commission, understood the nuances of the scheme. It was the support from such organisations that enabled the smooth rollout of the scheme.

Still, the RSBY happened

The National Commission for Enterprises in the Unorganised Sector (NCEUS) had produced a comprehensive report on providing social security to workers in the unorganised sector. It focussed on what was to be done rather than how it would be done. Perhaps the more difficult bit was defining the 'how' because what had been prescribed was extremely difficult, if not impossible, to translate into action. Subscription and collection of INR 1 per day from unorganised workers was one such example. The feasibility of implementation was not even discussed. The report dealt with diagnosis and prescription only. The diagnosis was perfunctory and the prescription without details. It ignored the fact that such prescriptions had failed in the past. There was no attempt to go into the causes of such failures. The report articulated a long wish list without trying to seriously suggest an implementable road map. The report did serve some purpose though. It became a handy tool for those who wanted to badger the government. They belonged to those groups that wanted everything but got nothing as they were not prepared to settle for anything short of everything.

Yet, the RSBY happened because of a dedicated set of people in these very ministries and departments. They ignored the departmental approach and found the RSBY attractive enough to give it all possible assistance. There were many who derived satisfaction by contributing to the evolution of the scheme without expecting anything in return. On occasions, they were not only dissuaded, but also ridiculed as they slogged selflessly to make the RSBY happen. It was inexplicable but true. Perhaps, Maslow was right. These disparate but committed officers were seeking 'self-actualisation' in the success of the RSBY.

The insurance people: Important characters

'What is needed is a better approach to help the poor, an approach that involves partnering with them to innovate and achieve sustainable win-win scenarios where the poor are actively engaged and, at the same time, the companies providing products and services to them are profitable. When the poor at the Bottom of Pyramid [BOP] are treated as consumers, they can reap the benefits of respect, choice, and self-esteem and have an opportunity to climb out of the poverty trap'.—C K Prahalad in *The Fortune at the Bottom of the Pyramid.*

At the outset, the insurance companies did not believe that such a scheme on such a scale would ever roll out. They were not only unprepared but also unwilling to prepare. Primarily operating in the comfortable confines of urban areas, investing time, effort and money in such an ambitious scheme was not their cup of tea. A series of meetings and a lot of groundwork had to be undertaken to convince the insurance companies that the government meant business and that there was a business for insurance companies in the scheme. Unlike other insurance schemes of the government that involved only public sector insurance companies, with an accompanying mandate from the concerned ministry, the RSBY was a scheme thrown in as a business proposition. Hence, it had to be marketed and sold.

The insurance companies were not technically well equipped to handle such a complex scheme, which needed a considerable amount of technical inputs. Initially, there was a new face in every meeting. These faces primarily represented public sector insurance companies. Most of them hardly took part in the discussion and when they did, they asked the most rudimentary of questions. The attitude was appalling. In the early stages, only one public sector insurance company and a couple of private sector companies showed interest.

The representative of one public sector insurance company repeatedly sought clarification about the relevance and the role of Third-Party Administrators (TPAs) under the RSBY in a number of meetings despite a response to his satisfaction on each occasion. He apparently had a set of questions which he kept repeating each time. Public sector companies also suffered because of centralisation of decision making as almost every decision was referred to the headquarters. Things changed gradually. At least a couple of them set up in-house teams to reduce their dependence on TPAs. As high claim ratios started pinching them, they woke up. One public sector insurance company, owned entirely by the central government took a state government to court, thereby stalling the entire process of rollout. The company lost the case but the real loss was of the beneficiaries who were deprived of the benefits under the scheme for more than a year.

A number of insurance companies participated in the bidding process without the necessary groundwork. Despite the highly technical nature of the scheme, technical teams were not involved in either understanding the nuances of the scheme or in the decision-making process. A large number of tasks were left to the TPAs who themselves had not been exposed to such a scheme in the past. It was chaotic to begin with, but a couple of insurance companies showed the way. They were prepared to invest time, money and effort as they saw an opportunity in this challenge. The problems were manifold and ranged from understanding the complex conceptual framework, procuring the hardware, putting human resources in place in inhospitable conditions, grappling with intransigent bureaucracy in some of the states to a host of technical issues. Yet people like Vijay Thakur of ICICI Lombard (who moved to a different company subsequently and did equally well there) never gave up. He was supported whole-heartedly by a visionary—MD of ICICI Lombard, Bhargav Dasgupta. Apollo Munich was a new company on the horizon but its Managing Director, Antony Jacob was never shy of experimenting. He was class apart. Chandrakant Mishra of Cholamandalam perceived the 'fortune lying at the bottom of the pyramid'. Monika Pusha of Royal Sundaram even assisted the central team in evolving certain modules. Shalabh Singhal of IFFCO-TOKIO clearly demonstrated that through sheer hard work a new company could also do well. R S Madan and Usha Solanki of Oriental Insurance proved that good work could be done in public sector companies as well though rewards were not as many. So was the case with Debjani Nath of National Insurance Corporation in West Bengal and Usha Girish of United India who made the best of the congenial environment in Kerala. There were other officers as well who displayed unflinching commitment. The RSBY would always be indebted to the likes of Sanjay Pande and Surabhi Chawla who provided extremely useful inputs during the formative years of the scheme.

Over a period, certain institutions evolved for the purpose of formal and informal interactions with insurance companies. The NaNOs (National Nodal Officers) representing each insurance company at the national level provided an effective interface in the evolution of the scheme. The monthly meetings were marked by open discussions and meaningful communication. The NaNOs grew in stature as did the institution. These monthly meetings also gave the insurance companies an opportunity to exchange notes and to learn from each other. Quarterly meetings with the Chairman and Managing Directors (CMDs) of the insurance companies served the purpose of engaging them in discussions that facilitated mid-course corrections at the policy level. Such interactions also helped in further strengthening the institution of NaNOs.

Hospitals: A huge opportunity beckoned the investors

For the first time in the history of the country, both public and private sector hospitals were engaged in the insurance network. The public sector hospitals took time to grasp the scope and details. The complexity of the scheme and the commitment needed were unprecedented. Officials had to be identified and trained in the use of technology. Purchase and installation of hardware and software for the transaction of business under the RSBY posed a great challenge. However, what was unique and, hence, difficult to understand was the receipt of funds from the insurance companies. Having followed government procedures in the past, they had no experience of handling funds independently, as a society. The institution of *Rogi Kalyan Samiti* under NRHM came handy. However, the shortage of staff and, in some cases, overcrowding of public hospitals created their own problems.

The private sector hospitals had a distinct set of problems. The larger 'five-star' hospitals found the rates very low for them to indulge in the service of the poor. They had thrived in the commercial business of making money like any other business, and the business opportunity under the RSBY was not attractive enough. The medium and small hospitals appreciated the scheme but took time to understand the technology. Adoption of the technology was also quite challenging. Not all could appreciate the 'business' proposition in the scheme as there was significant initial investment involved in setting up hardware and software.

Some of the states did not have a network of private hospitals. The RSBY allowed the beneficiaries to go to any network hospital anywhere in the country. It was hoped that the RSBY would incentivise setting up of private hospitals in remote areas. To everyone's relief, private hospitals did come up in remote areas.

An enabling provision was created for the government-owned Employee State Insurance Corporation (ESIC) to take part in the RSBY by way of providing health services to the beneficiaries. However, unlike the monopoly which the ESIC had with regards to IPs (Insured Persons), under the RSBY, the ESIC had to compete with the other public and private hospitals to attract consumers. The ESIC was ill-equipped in terms of facilities (doctors, infrastructure) and attitude.

It was imperative to ensure that all the stakeholders were on board. As the RSBY came out of the blue for some of them, it took them some time and a lot of persuasion to own the scheme. However, after that, there was no looking back.

Marketing of the RSBY: The next big challenge for the central government

The RSBY was one of the most ambitious health insurance schemes ever undertaken by the Government of India. However, there is a difference between a well-designed scheme and a well-accepted one. It was found that well-planned marketing efforts would be desirable given the complexity of the scheme and on account of a large number of stakeholders involved. The list included the government bodies (both at the centre and in the state), the insurance companies, the smart card service providers, the health service providers, the intermediaries and the beneficiaries.

The product RSBY was created by the central government and not by an insurance company. Hence, the primary responsibility of 'marketing' this product lay with the officials of the central government. It was believed that if there was an incentive system built into the design of the scheme for different stakeholders, then marketing would be comparatively less difficult. Keeping this in mind, the scheme was designed as a 'business model' with inbuilt business incentives for the key stakeholders.

The insurance companies had an incentive to issue as many cards as possible as they got the payment based on the number of beneficiaries they would enrol. This was at variance with the earlier approaches where the money was given in advance to an insurance company and the entire target group was insured at one go. Under the RSBY, the hospitals too had the incentive to accept patients as the payment was assured. Thus, attending to the poorest of the poor became a business proposition for the hospitals as well. They were just unearthing 'the fortune lying at the bottom of the pyramid'. Even in the case of smart card service providers, there were business opportunities available in the sheer volumes on a long-term basis.

This scheme gave the state governments an opportunity to launch a well-designed product for which they had to spend only 25% of the cost without the hassles of planning, designing etc. The scheme, as the states gradually discovered, made a lot of 'political sense' as well. In fact, some states found so much value in the scheme that they extended the scheme beyond the categories of workers that were funded by the central government.

Despite the potential business opportunities, the reluctance on the part of some of the key players was natural because of the negative perception of government schemes and upfront investments involved to procure hardware, to develop software and to put in place the required manpower. The complexity of the scheme, the commitment required in terms of time and finances, and the preconceived notion that the social sector was an exclusive domain of the government were major deterrents in accepting a scheme like the RSBY which promotes the public-private partnership. This state of things mandated a marketing campaign.

The scheme was initially 'marketed' through a well-defined strategy. Attempts were made to involve all the stakeholders at various stages. Right from the design stage to implementation, stakeholders were consulted and brought on board.

At the policy formulation stage, video conferences were held with the state governments and documents were shared. The initiatives taken by the top officers proved the unflinching commitment of the central government. A series of interactive sessions were held with the insurance companies. Many of their concerns were addressed during these interactions. These efforts enabled inculcation of some sense of ownership amongst some, if not all, of the stakeholders.

Once the policy was announced, senior officers of the central government visited as many as 20 states to 'market' the scheme through intensive interactions. This also gave an opportunity to gather state-specific details and reservations against the proposed approach, as also an occasion to provide clarity about various aspects which facilitated dispelling of misapprehensions. The central government remained accessible to the states seeking clarifications and responded to communications promptly. Assistance was provided to the states, both in terms of understanding of the technology as well as organising workshops at various levels. Documents and templates (like the draft tender document and contract document) were standardised to facilitate the launch of the scheme. Capacities were developed at the central level to be able to assist the states.

Apart from that, organisations like the World Bank, GIZ, National Informatics Centre (NIC) and Standardisation Testing and Quality Certification (STQC) were approached for evolving standardised technical documents and to develop capacity.

At the implementation stage, the states were given guidance to prepare documents related to the processes. They were given assistance not only to launch the scheme but also to organise state-level workshops. Similarly, technical assistance, in the form of necessary software and usage training, was extended to the states as well. The marketing effort paid dividends. The scheme was positioned as a win-win model for all the stakeholders. The stakeholders came to 'own' the scheme and this made a huge difference. There were a lot of problems as was expected in a scheme of this scale, but those were seen as 'our' problem rather than 'my' or 'your' problem. Hence, more often than not, solutions were forthcoming.

Getting the states on board: Difficult terrain

The response of the states to the scheme ranged from indifferent to hostile. Because of the complex nature of the scheme, marketing became the biggest challenge. Some states did not want to make any financial contribution. They expected the centre to bear the entire burden. The other states had an ongoing health insurance scheme and did not find it necessary to seek assistance from the centre. The bureaucracy in some of the states did not find it important to roll out the new scheme. Subsequently, the issue was settled at the political level with the concerned bureaucrats taken to task. However, it was the political leadership that became a roadblock in another state on ideological grounds. Here, the bureaucracy was keen on pushing the scheme. A few states saw the scheme as imperative for the poor and got going right away. In such cases, there was support both at the bureaucratic and political level. The back-end complexity of the scheme and the effort needed to roll it out dissuaded a number of bureaucrats. But, the real problem came from such bureaucrats who thought that they already knew everything.

The desert state of western India had the distinction of being one of the first few states to implement the RSBY. The excitement during the first state-level workshop was palpable. Collectors of the selected districts appeared extremely enthusiastic and the scheme was driven by a committed bureaucrat, Roli Singh. After a few initial hiccups, the smart cards started rolling out. In fact, the insurance company had already issued more than one lakh smart cards when the trouble started. The state went overboard in the first year, fascinated with the idea of a smart card and the potential it had. It was then that they began to hijack the scheme. They came up with their own so-called omnibus scheme and wanted to subsume the RSBY within it. The state and its bureaucracy did not even care to go into the details. Under the pressure to do 'anything' in an election year, the bureaucrats promised 'everything' to the political masters, going to the extent of creating numerous roadblocks in the ongoing rollout of the RSBY. The state government, thus, announced the Bhamashah Scheme using smart cards to dole out INR 1500 to each BPL family. However, in the context of the RSBY, a battle ensued between the centre and the state. The roll-out of smart cards under the RSBY was halted by the state as the debate raged. Necessary spadework was not done with regards to either technology or operations for launching the Bhamashah Scheme. The incumbent ruling party lost the assembly elections. The Bhamashah Scheme met with the same fate as did the RSBY which came to be associated with the 'discredited scheme'. However, the poor community of the state were the biggest sufferers as they lost out on health insurance coverage due to the intransigence of the state-level bureaucracy and the shortsightedness of the politicians. It took more than three years for the scheme to be revived in the state.

Then there were states where the only industry thriving was the 'transfer industry'. The RSBY suffered because of frequent transfers of the key persons who were sensitised about the scheme in the state. Little could be done about this, but it was a major challenge. They performed like a yoyo. It did well when those in charge of the scheme in the state were committed but floundered when the bureaucrats in charge of the scheme were reluctant participants. Some collectors in those states still retained a feudal mentality. They treated the RSBY like any other scheme and the scheme suffered as it needed more facilitation and less monitoring. When the scheme started moving, someone discovered that even this scheme could be 'milked'. A decision was taken to shift the scheme from the Rural Development Department to the Health Department though there were doubts about the health of the new department.

In another state, it was difficult to understand the loopholes because everything went wrong. The bureaucracy was indifferent. Then, the courts got into action. When the courts relented, a bureaucrat became hostile. It was administration at its worst; any one individual could hold back the entire process. Repeated requests to shift the scheme to a more willing and equipped department in the state were ignored. The decision-makers were oblivious of the fact that all around the country; the scheme was thriving, helping thousands of subscribers. Those in this state were busy creating their own battlefields even as the poor suffered.

Yet another government in another state was obsessed with itself. Several bureaucrats as well felt that the left was always right. Hence, they sought to find problems with anything that came from elsewhere. Consequently, even though the RSBY was meant for the poorest of the poor, the scheme took a long time to roll out in the state. And, when it did, the process was riddled with snags. It was never clear who would be in charge. The local politics made matters worse. There was virtual paralysis of analysis and the scheme rolled out in fits and starts. However, despite the stumbling blocks, the scheme picked up and the state gradually emerged as one of the finest performing states in the country. It happened as the utility of the scheme finally dawned on the functionaries of the state government.

Mr Nitish Kumar was making a huge effort to turn around the state of Bihar and was being lauded for his effort. However, the bureaucracy, at least some part of it, was still to emerge from the feudal past. Difficult terrain, the absence of institutions and an aggressive set of bureaucrats made the roll-out of the scheme extremely difficult. More often than not, the team was busy finding faults rather than solutions. No one seemed to have time to read the finer details of such a complex scheme. This led to a lot of confusion and bitterness on several occasions. Some of the stakeholders were terrified of the senior bureaucrats who discouraged open discussions. The scheme had evolved and thrived on such discussions, but it was different in Bihar. Hence, the scheme suffered. In many cases, cards were not distributed on the spot after enrolments, as mandated under the scheme. There was hardly any attempt to analyse the problem dispassionately. Therefore, the solutions were not forthcoming.

Kerala emerged as one of the finest performers under the scheme, in terms of both enrolment and hospitalisation. However, a central scheme was not palatable in the prescribed form. The left government dithered in the beginning and wanted its stamp on the scheme, somehow. The scheme promoted competition and was market-driven. This was an anathema to the state government. The changes that were suggested by the state to suit their ideology would have derailed the entire scheme. Discussion at the level of the then Chief Minister did not cut much ice. He dozed off even as the nuances of the scheme were being explained to him. What finally clinched the issue was the meeting that took place between Dr B Mungekar, Member, Planning Commission, the State Finance Minister and the Chairman, State Planning Board. However, even these parleys were not smooth and, at one point in time, it seemed as if the whole exercise was abandoned. The Union Labour Secretary who belonged to the same cadre gave up and left. Once she left, the state representatives were told that they had to make a choice of either accepting the scheme as it stood or forgo the assistance that was being made available under the scheme. They were also candidly informed about the potential loss in case the scheme was not implemented in the state.

It is still a mystery how the State Finance Minister not only agreed with the proposition but also considered extending it to the scheme to the Above Poverty Line (APL) persons as well.

Then, the state got so enamoured of the scheme that it not only extended it to all the districts, but also a decision was taken to extend it to such families who were not recognised as BPL by the central government. Whereas 75% of the premium contribution for the centrally recognised BPL families came from the central government, the state agreed to foot the entire bill for such families who were not funded by the central government. The scheme was implemented well in the state because of a proactive bureaucracy led by an energetic State Labour Secretary, Vishwanathan, and an extremely effective head of State Nodal Agency, P Sukumar. The State Labour Minister bypassed the protocol and came down to the hotel to meet the Union Labour Secretary to break an impasse that threatened to derail the scheme. His pleasing demeanour and willingness to find solutions went a long way in giving a solid foundation to the scheme in the state. Though the scheme was being administered by the State Labour Department, the Health Department extended all possible assistance. Dinesh Arora, a bright young IAS officer in the Health Department, led from the front. Thus, all the government hospitals were empanelled under the scheme and a management graduate was appointed in each district hospital as a Public Relations Officer to handle it. This was the only state in the country to have enrolled more than 1 million families in the first year, and thousands of beneficiaries availed cashless hospitalisation service. The scheme made a massive impact in the state and still continues to do so.

The bureaucracy in the NCT of Delhi epitomised callous indifference. The officers of the state treated the RSBY like any other government scheme hoping that it would just happen by itself. The then State Labour Secretary stayed at the crucial state level workshop only during the inaugural session and made a regal departure along with the Minister as soon as the session was over.

Lack of commitment was evident, and the scheme did not take off during the first year. The scheme entailed a lot of coordination but that was the last thing in the minds of those who were administering the scheme in the state. The administrators were busy advertising the scheme in national dailies, including the English ones, when not much was happening on the ground. The scheme was virtually grounded even before it took off in the state. Though the scheme earned encomiums in other parts of the country, it wilted right under the nose of the central government. All the international teams that arrived in India were whisked away to other states to see how the scheme was doing. It was a matter of shame, but no one seemed to be bothered.

Karnataka was a classic example of our inability to realise the potential of the scheme. The state has made a name for itself in promoting IT applications. However, in the hands of some bureaucrats, it became one of the biggest handicaps. There was a feeling of having 'arrived' and, hence, there was nothing new to learn. The RSBY was based on IT applications and of course no outsider could teach Karnataka how to use such applications. Consequently, nothing happened. Matters became worse on account of the intransigence of bureaucrats in the State Health Department who had a closed mind and were not even prepared to listen. Eventually, the concerned bureaucrat was moved out, but it cost an otherwise progressive state one full year.

The North-Eastern states were laid-back. The bureaucratic apathy and indifference were appalling. Chief Secretary of one of the states admitted having been overawed by the scheme and expressed his inability to travel the distance. In another state, the bureaucracy always said 'yes' to everything and did nothing. A senior bureaucrat in one of the states was fond of travelling to Delhi. Discussions related to the RSBY became a convenient platform, but he did not do anything after these discussions. The bureaucracy here was often elusive, evasive, and indifferent; sufficient explanation for the backwardness of the region despite the copious flow of funds from the centre. However, Nagaland stood apart. It became the first state to roll out the scheme in the Northeast. It happened because of the untiring perseverance of a young Yanger, a junior officer. He single-handedly made the scheme happen in Nagaland. It became an example for the other states in the region. Later, states, like Tripura, also came to appreciate the value of the scheme.

Haryana, a Congress-ruled state, was one of the first few states to begin the implementation of the scheme. As expected there were numerous teething troubles, but the state officials never gave up. They clearly proved that it could be done. The task was indeed a difficult one. The scheme was complex and required unflinching bureaucratic commitment and political support. The scheme happened in Haryana as the state 'owned' it and found value in what was sought to be delivered. Consequently, around 600,000 smart cards were distributed in the first year itself. The enthusiasm at the field level had to be seen to be believed. Dr Saharan, Director ESI and in-charge for the scheme in the state, led the way with the infectious enthusiasm of a young man though he had just a couple of years to go before retirement. The scheme entailed coordination among various stakeholders. This was accomplished through dialogue, motivation, accommodation and a positive attitude. The Bill Gates team visited the state and saw enrolment sites and termed it a 'very impressive sight to behold'. The state had set benchmarks for others, both in terms of enrolment as well as hospitalisation. The utilisation rate in the first district that completed one year was more than 80% though there was some concern in this context in the second one.

There were many lessons to be learnt from what happened in Haryana. Here was a state that was not afraid of taking a plunge into the unchartered territory of a complex technology-driven health insurance scheme and it succeeded. More than that, it showed to the other initially reluctant states that the RSBY could happen though it did require a lot of hard work and perseverance. The BJP was in power in the state of Gujarat. But, it did not matter. They too found value in the scheme once they understood its nuances. Despite starting late, the state soon emerged in the forefront, issuing around 700,000 smart cards during the first year of the scheme. The state bureaucracy was professional in its approach and got down to business once the government took a decision. Led by the inimitable State Health Commissioner, Dr Amarjeet Singh and ably aided by Vijendre Katre, a clear-headed and result-oriented bureaucrat, the scheme got cracking, using innovative ways of project monitoring. Gujarat soon became an example to other states as their teams started visiting to ascertain and learn from what was being done there. Realising the utility of the scheme, a decision was taken by the state government to extend the scheme to all the districts in the state during the first year.

It was not clear who was running the state at the political level as governments kept changing in the state of Jharkhand. The state was not a known performer in terms of implementation of development schemes. The terrain was difficult. Left Wing Extremism (LWE) affected several districts. However, none of these factors could prevent a set of bureaucrats from launching the RSBY in the state, making it a success and setting an example not only for the eastern states but also for the entire country. The initial hurdles were taken care of by an unassuming but persevering Sushil Choudhary. Aradhana Patnaik, an extremely effective bureaucrat, then picked up the gauntlet. Fighting against all odds, they made the scheme 'happen' in the state. It happened in the districts where few government schemes had penetrated. This demonstrated that given the desired commitment, all hurdles could be overcome.

There were various other problems. And these varied across states depending upon the nature of the civil servant that headed the department and the politician to whom he reported. However, intensive engagement with the states enabled the resolution of most of the issues. It was a pleasure travelling to remote parts of the country, to states one had never visited in the past. It was a unique marketing challenge. The journey was tough but extremely enjoyable. The best bit was that ultimately most of the states came on board.

The RSBY was rolled out in most of the states of the country, irrespective of the political hue of the government. At the top, in terms of performance, lay four states, all governed by different political parties at that point in time. But, it did not really matter whether the government belonged to the Left, the Right, the centre or somewhere else. And, in this sense, the rollout of the scheme was not inhibited by political ideologies. One of the reasons for the initial success of the scheme was its apolitical nature. Ironically, the scheme made a lot of political sense. The scheme generated a lot of interest and held the potential of being one of the best in terms of transparent delivery of tangible benefits to the poorest of the poor in the country as also for providing an IT platform for other such schemes.

Taking the RSBY to town

We experienced a wave of rising expectations after the initial success of the RSBY. The media had been kind to the scheme, in the initial years. This was also on account of the fact that no effort was made to declare that the scheme had arrived. Everyone was allowed to experience it themselves.

Virendra Kumar, one of the beneficiaries under the scheme, called it 'great' but for the scheme to really become great, the focus had to be on the process. Most of the government schemes focus on 'launches', 'foundation stones', 'publicity' and 'targets' because that brings in immediate kudos. However, most of them fail eventually because the process is not 'exciting' enough for those who implement the scheme. The RSBY followed a different route. It tried to overcome the temptation of 'launches' and 'targets' that relate to pure numbers.

There are various organisations in the government that spend millions of rupees on advertisements without making a commensurate effort to improve the product quality because terms like 'product quality' or 'service quality' are not really understood in the bureaucratic parlance. These advertisements accomplish some narcissist pursuits but hardly anything beyond it. There have been few efforts to objectively ascertain the requirements of the target audience and an analysis of the impact these expensive advertisements have on this audience. Fortunately, the RSBY did not fall into this trap. The approach for the RSBY was simple. Focus on the quality of service and the process of delivery, and the beneficiaries themselves would advertise it enough. In any case, what the beneficiary said about the scheme would carry more weight as compared to what was portrayed in advertisements. There was also a concerted effort to provide all the information to those seeking it. This included the journalists. Transparency helped and criticism, if any, was taken in the right spirit. It was treated as useful feedback in improving the process. It was clear that as the scheme reached out to more and more people, it would be open to increased scrutiny.

The Times of India followed the initial accolades showered by *The Wall Street Journal* where Gurcharan Das, in a piece written on 1 November 2008, rated the scheme as 'the best Diwali present'.

Gradually the scheme came to be recognised by other sections of the media as *The Hindu* in its editorial on 19 November 2008 called the scheme, 'a smart approach to public health'. *The Hindustan Times* came up with a full-page feature on the scheme on 5 July 2010 and commented that, 'the master card revolution has delivered cashless, paperless healthcare to 60 million people per INR 30. It is the largest system in the world'. Subsequently, even *India Today* in its annual edition of 2010, stated that 'The Rashtriya Swasthya Bima Yojana (RSBY) has transformed the lives of over 65 million people in the unorganised sector'. *The Economic Times* in a news item on 20 May 2011 announced that, 'The Rashtriya Swasthya Bima Yojana is now attracting a slew of entrepreneurs to set up hospitals primarily targeted at the rural poor'.

The British Broadcasting Cooperation came out with a feature on the RSBY based on the evidence that they had gathered. It was indicated that, 'It's a government effort and it seems to be working and that the government seems to have a winning model with the first market-driven welfare scheme'.

The media was kind. The strategy seemed to have worked. Sharing information and encouraging scrutiny had helped. The scheme benefitted from an open approach. The product could speak for itself. The focus had initially been on evaluation and introspection with a view to improving the processes. No conscious effort was made to go to town on advertising the scheme, but it announced itself, without a single penny having been spent on advertising.

The motivation behind the RSBY:
From the depths of my heart

I was on a visit to the World Bank for a presentation on the RSBY before a select audience. During this visit in the US, a Washington-based organisation—Brookings Institute, invited me to talk about the scheme to another set of audience comprising government representatives, non-governmental organisation and some funding agencies like the Bill Gates Foundation. The presentation went smoothly and was apparently received well. However, what is etched in my memory is the informal conversation with a representative of a foundation during the tea break. The question he posed was quite simple, "Mr Swarup, why are you so passionate about the scheme? What are you getting out of it?" I took a while to respond. It was clear that during my presentation, I had conveyed a level of commitment to the scheme that was beyond the expectation from a thoroughbred bureaucrat. I countered him, "What do you get when you part with millions of dollars to help the poor in developing countries?" His response did not surprise me, "That is our job and our purpose. We additionally get a lot of good wishes from those that are assisted by us". He now awaited my response. My answer was simple and came from the depth of my heart, "I am better off than you. I don't spend a single penny from my pocket, yet all the good wishes and blessings from the poor benefitting under the scheme come back to me. What could be a better motivation!" and then I narrated an incident to illustrate my point.

Blessings from a beneficiary: The best award so far

"*Beta, Idhar Aao*" (Come here my son)—a feeble voice called me as I stood in a Delhi hospital. I was there to check on a patient. Turning around I found an old lady lying in a bed nearby. She waved and signaled me to go over to her. As I approached, I saw an emaciated figure that looked weak and haggard. She tried to get up but could not. The pain was writ large on her face, but she greeted me with a smile. Someone had told her that I was associated with the RSBY. She had the RSBY smart card in her hand and she was flashing it to me. As I enquired about her welfare, she confessed that she was in pain but conveyed her appreciation for the hospital staff that had looked after her very well despite her inability to pay a single penny to them, as she was poor. She seemed resigned to her fate as she admitted that time had come for her to meet the Almighty. But, I wasn't prepared for what came next. She was all praise for the scheme and she said that she would convey this to the Almighty when she would meet Him and seek His blessings for the scheme. Gradually she gathered her strength to sit up and raised her hand to bless me. The scheme had won several awards but this one was the best.

Poor calculation: Still Punjab welcomed the RSBY

The then Chief Minister of Punjab was in Delhi. I was informed that he wanted a brief discussion on the RSBY at once. I got barely 15 minutes to reach Kapurthala House.

The scheme was in its infancy and I did not want to lose this opportunity. I was, in any case, travelling all over the country to market the scheme. While confirming the invitation, I requested a projector so that a powerpoint presentation could be made. On arrival at Kapurthala House, I found everything handy and delivered the presentation within 30 minutes. The audience consisted of the Chief Minister, his Principal Secretary and the Resident Commissioner. One could not make out from the expressionless face of the CM whether the presentation had made an impact or not. There was a short pause. Then he asked a few truly relevant questions related to the efficacy of the scheme. I answered them one by one. His face was still impassive. Then, he asked the final question, "What amount of money would be required annually to cover the entire BPL population?" I made some back-of-the-envelope calculation instantly and informed him that there would be a requirement of around INR 60 crore. He immediately asked his Principal Secretary to put him through to the Finance Secretary on the phone (still with an expressionless face!). When connected, he issued a clear direction in chaste Punjabi to the officer to earmark INR 60 crore for the scheme. I was thrilled because the RSBY had found footing in yet another state. On returning to the office, I looked at the calculation and discovered that the amount needed was only INR 6 crore and not INR 60 crore.

Anyway, the scheme got moving in the state. Despite teething troubles during the first year, the state soon emerged as one of the finest performers. It happened in the state because it did not take long for the CM to gauge the value that the scheme could provide. For him, INR 60 crore or INR 6 crores did not really matter. He put together a certain set of bureaucrats to make the scheme happen ... and it did happen.

The first card: Haryana got the ticket

They say that the first step is the most difficult. The RSBY took a while to get going. Most of the government schemes face similar hurdles and fail because the focus is usually on the 'launching' of a new scheme (in this case the smart card) and not so much on its efficacy. Despite repeated failures of the earlier smart card projects in the government domain, a mandate was issued to 'launch' the smart card on 2 October 2007. The necessary groundwork was not done. Hence, the powers-that-be were told that this was not possible. This caused a lot of unpleasantness, but the bullet had to be bitten in the long-term interest of the scheme. The officers that resisted the move suffered for some time but the scheme benefitted.

The first card was handed over in the remote village Chapar in Yamunanagar District in Haryana on 28 February 2008 without much fanfare. This was the first of the millions of smart cards issued under the RSBY. Ironically, those that were managing another government scheme succumbed to the pressure and issued 500 smart cards on 2 October 2007. This launch gave a great photo opportunity. However, these turned out to be the last set of smart cards issued under that scheme as was the case in a number of such ventures launched by the government. The RSBY was an exception.

The Chief Minister intervened: The RSBY rolled out successfully in all the districts

The reluctance of the state government in Chhattisgarh to implement the scheme was clear. No one was prepared to touch the scheme with a barge pole. The scheme was too complex for them. The Principal Secretary of the State Labour Department questioned the poor beneficiaries' ability to use these 'electronic gizmos' (alluding to the smart card). The scheme demanded hard work and it was evident that some of the bureaucrats were not prepared to put in additional hours and efforts needed to get it going.

When all else seemed to have failed, a final effort was made. I sought appointment from the Chief Secretary of the State. The meeting took place in Raipur and I travelled all the way. But, the Chief Secretary too conveyed the same reluctance in rolling out this 'complex' scheme. It was quite exasperating. The state and its poor population were in dire need of the RSBY that could have taken care of their health needs, but the bureaucracy was reluctant to put in arduous work. However, I was determined not to give up. I sought time to meet the then Chief Minister. Luckily, he acknowledged my request and gave me five minutes from his busy schedule. As I was ushered to his office, Dr Raman Singh appeared relaxed and heard me out for five minutes as I tried to convey to him the value of the RSBY. I could see that he was focussed and did not utter a single word until I had completed my presentation. I did not tell him about the reluctance of the state bureaucracy in implementing the scheme. But, during the presentation, I had conveyed to him that the central government was prepared to extend the scheme to one-fifth of the districts during the first year.

Having listened to me, he asked a simple question, "Can't the scheme be extended to all the districts of the state in the first year?" He was a doctor by profession and in five minutes he had understood the importance of the RSBY. He was not deterred by the 'electronic gizmos'. The next one hour spent with him was amazing as he summoned the senior officers of the state government and explained to them why the RSBY should be implemented in the state and in all the districts.

The state performed brilliantly and earned the status of 'mentor' state to help an adjoining state that rolled out the scheme much later.

'Home' was calling: I preferred to stay in 'Labour'

"Are you aware that you have been posted as Additional Secretary, Home?", one of my batchmates telephoned and asked me late in the evening. It took me some time to absorb the question. I could not believe it. I had just turned down a lucrative World Bank offer for an assignment to continue with the RSBY journey. Ironically, the government was being criticised on many fronts and the RSBY was one of the very few reasons for it to hold its head high. Given this backdrop, I was shocked. I at once spoke to the Minister and the Labour Secretary (both of them had become fond of the RSBY by now and recognised the contribution that I was making towards it). A flurry of letters and discussions at various levels followed this conversation. There was some initial reluctance at the bureaucratic level, but both the Secretary and the Minister refused to relieve me despite the pressure from 'Home'. Finally, the order was rescinded but not before a loss of three weeks. I had never attempted to get my transfer order changed in my entire career in the past other than this. It was done in the interest of the RSBY as I preferred to stay 'in labour' and not go 'home'!

Pakistan welcomed the RSBY: Kashmir issue could have been resolved

It was a World Bank initiative and the venue was Bangkok. The separated twins (India and Pakistan) hardly spoke to each other. And, when they did, it was more often than not through the barrel of a gun. The two countries had evolved differently. Whereas democratic traditions and maturing institutions had made India proud, the counterpart had already been split and was still struggling (often failing) to evolve as a democracy. However, like natural twins, there were many common features. The two countries had similarities in culture, geography and poverty. There was indeed a growing concern for the poor. The RSBY was happening in India and was favourably impacting the lives of the poor by giving cashless inpatient healthcare. At least some in Pakistan were keen to learn from this experiment.

More than a dozen representatives from the federal and state governments from Pakistan, along with senior officials, were taking part in the workshop with the primary objective of learning from the Indian experience. After a presentation on the RSBY, they all seemed to agree that a similar approach should be adopted in Pakistan. However, there were differences of opinion between the federal representatives and the state government secretaries on how it was to be rolled out there. Whereas the federal government representatives were strongly of the view that the programme should be directly funded and implemented by the centre, the states were adamant that though the funding should come from the centre, the implementation should be left to the states. The team from India managed to convince the 'warring' factions that the scheme should jointly be implemented as well as funded by the centre and the states as was done in India. This would ensure 'ownership' at each level which was essential for success.

It was interesting that an Indian was trying to bring about a reconciliation between two sets of strong views within Pakistan. The mission was accomplished without much rancour. Both the parties from Pakistan displayed faith in this Indian who was 'arbitrating' between them. By the end of the second day, the bonhomie reached such levels that made me believe that even the Kashmir issue, if handed over to this group, could be resolved.

Award but no award: Permission not granted

"I am delighted to inform you that the 'Healthcare personality of the Year Award' is being conferred to you", was the message from the Secretary-General, Federation of Indian Chambers of Commerce and Industry (FICCI), one of the premier industry associations in the country. This award was being conferred as a mark of recognition for the remarkable work that I had done over the years through the RSBY, which had transformed the lives of millions of people in the unorganised sector. The contribution was termed as 'path-breaking approach to healthcare delivery'. The communication went on to state that the scheme had then become a model for other public programmes. None other than the redoubtable Mr M Damodaran, Former Chairman, SEBI, UTI and IDBI headed the jury.

The award ceremony was scheduled to be held on 2 September 2013. This necessitated a response from the government on 22 August 2013 on receipt of intimation from the FICCI. The government that was being criticised and badgered on most of the fronts could have seized this opportunity and taken credit for having launched a scheme that was transforming the lives of millions. However, it chose not to. An enigmatic message received from an undersecretary on 2 September (the day on which the award was to be given) mentioned that the grant of permission to accept the award was 'under consideration in consultation with the Department of Personnel & Training'. Consequently, much to everyone's embarrassment, the FICCI was informed that the award would not be accepted as necessary permission had not been received from the government. It was ironical that despite being responsible for 'fast-tracking' stalled projects entailing an investment of INR 1,000 crores or more, I was unable to 'fast-track' the permission to accept an award that would have brought much-needed recognition to the then-beleaguered government.

Humane Stories

The young man

It was cold but not enough to wear gloves inside a room. The young man who walked into my room was wearing a glove, only on his left hand.

I had this unusual habit of reaching office half an hour ahead of the scheduled time and one normally did not expect a visitor so early. In fact, the whole idea of coming early was to plan for the day without being disturbed. Being a public servant and being accessible had its own problems. It was difficult to find time to plan and think of new ideas. There were meetings, phone calls and visitors right through the day. The initial half an hour before the commencement of formal proceedings provided that space and time—to think, to innovate, to plan and to reflect. However, the scene was different that day in the office of Registrar, Co-operative Societies where I was posted as Additional Registrar, Banking.

The young man appeared confident despite a pale countenance. He wanted a few minutes from me. I felt irritated but his persistence left me with no other option.

He had a strange story to narrate. He was an employee of a Co-operative Bank in a remote district but had eventually become a drug addict. He stole money to buy drugs and was caught. He was thrown out of the bank and now, he wanted his job back. I could do nothing in these set of circumstances, and I wondered why he had travelled the distance for such a ridiculous proposition. He perhaps sensed my reaction as he could read the expression on my face. However, he carried on unfazed and went on to narrate how he had suffered after being thrown out of the bank. The mystery of the single hand glove was unraveled as he took it off to display the artificial left hand. He had lost his hand because of gangrene. The injection needles to administer drugs had caused this. He later had successfully gone through the process of rehabilitation and wanted to be rehabilitated in the bank as well. His last statement was impressive. If he was not rehabilitated, he would either go back to drugs or commit suicide. His tone was neither threatening nor a pleading one. It betrayed conviction as he conveyed this as a matter of fact.

Despite a limited experience of six years in the administrative service, I knew that he was not lying and the case was genuine. It was still a huge risk and bureaucracy by definition is risk-averse. Anyway, I was prepared to stick my neck out. I asked the young man to pen down an application and then verified the details on telephone from the concerned bank. Then I initiated a note and took that to the Registrar who was the appointing authority. He looked at me incredulously as I narrated the story. Having worked with him for a while, he knew that I had no axe to grind but he was not sure whether I was doing the right thing. He still approved my proposal. The man who had lost his hand, found his job.

There was no news of this young man for the next couple of years. More importantly, no enquiry was initiated against me for having reinstated someone who had been a drug addict and was caught stealing. I moved out of the department (in those days we did not move as frequently as they did subsequently in Uttar Pradesh).

My daughter had inherited my crooked teeth and we were consulting an orthodontist for a 'repair' job. Most of the doctors take care of their patients but this one appeared to be taking extra care. When the job was done, we asked for the amount to be paid for the services. He simply smiled. As we insisted, he smiled again and narrated the story of the rehabilitation of the young man who happened to be his cousin. The doctor refused to take money from someone who had given a new lease of life to his cousin.

The 'young man' continued to do well for himself. He got married and settled. A few years down the line, he sent me a copy of *All The Prime Minister's Men* by Janardan Thakur. He indeed had a sense of humour.

The day I got my 'Bharat Ratna'

I could not resist keeping up with my 'bad' habit of reaching office early even when posted as the DM of Lakhimpur Kheri. DMs were generally known to operate from the precincts of their 'Camp Office'. I was seen as setting an 'unhealthy' precedent in arriving at the Collectorate ahead of the scheduled time. Perhaps they felt that I would change with the passage of time in the district. But, as they say, old habits die hard. In my case, they didn't die.

I encountered an aged couple in one of those early mornings at the Collectorate. The husband, as I later discovered, was blind and the wife was as good as blind. They had a usual story with an unusual demand. Nobody was there to support them and, without help, they would die of hunger. What they sought from me was not alms, but some money which could be used to buy plastic cord for knitting chairs. They could do nothing else to eke out a living but had the skill to knit. The sum requested by them was INR 100, which in the year 1991 was a reasonably substantial amount. Under normal circumstances, I would have normally not parted with this sum, as that was the only amount in my wallet. In any case, DMs are not known to throw money around. However, one could discern a determination in the couple to lead a meaningful existence. I gave them the money that I had. I would have survived without that money but for them it was critical.

The episode was soon forgotten, as was the money. Life carried on as unusually as ever in a district—with ravaging floods, the 'Ram-Mandir' agitation, an overnight encounter with the terrorists, the fallout of Mandal Commission and the like. Almost a year had gone by but my habit of reaching the Collectorate ahead of scheduled time had not changed. One day, I found the same couple standing there again, awaiting my arrival. The husband had a garland in his hand and his wife guided him to garland me the moment I alighted from the car. I couldn't really fathom what was going on. The couple had come to thank me for having saved their lives and also to return INR 100 which they had taken from me. It was incredible. I refused to take the money and garlanded the old man instead. I was poorer by INR 100 but I had won my Bharat Ratna that day.

Serving the Richest of the Rich

Head of the Project Monitoring Group: To serve the 'rich'

It was 2013. Everything was going wrong for the UPA II government. There were scams all around. Everyone, including civil servants, was on the run with enforcement agencies in hot pursuit. Consequently, no one had the time or inclination to take decisions. Investment had come to a grinding halt as necessary clearances were not coming through.

"Cabinet Secretary wants to speak to you urgently"—came a message as I landed at the IG International Airport after a visit to Siem Reap, Cambodia. I had gone there to discuss the RSBY. It was late in the evening yet I tried to reach the Cabinet Secretary on the phone, anticipating some 'news'. He asked me whether I could meet him early in the morning on the following day. I attempted to ascertain the context but his reply was cryptic though pleasant, "Just for a brief chat". Aware of the fact that the top bureaucrat would not just want a 'brief chat', I could barely sleep that night. My mind was cluttered with all sorts of thoughts.

Arriving ahead of the appointed hour at the Cabinet Secretariat housed in one corner of the Rashtrapati Bhawan (perhaps a colonial hangover as the Cabinet Secretariat has nothing to do with the Rashtrapati now), I awaited the arrival of the Cabinet Secretary with bated breath. I was more anxious than nervous. Even the Cabinet Secretary arrived early. As he walked through the corridor leading to his room, he spotted me sitting in the visitor's room. He waived and called me in.

"You have been drafted for a new assignment," he got down to business even before I could settle down. My mind was racing. A couple of years ago I was drafted to man the 'Naxal Division' in the Ministry of Home but the Labour Minister saw to it that I continued to serve the poorest of the poor through the RSBY. On this occasion, however, there couldn't be any such excuse as my extended tenure of seven years was coming to a close. I said to him, "Sir, I am completing my extended tenure. Hence, I will have to return to the state for mandatory 'cooling'". His response confounded me further, "You have been given extension of one more year". This was unusual. Maximum tenure for IAS officers on central deputation was for seven years and he had just announced an extension beyond that. My apprehensions grew, as I was still not aware what awaited me. As I looked incredulously at him, he revealed the nature of the assignment. With a view to fast-tracking stalled large investment projects, a Project Monitoring Group (PMG) was to be set up in the Cabinet Secretariat and I had been drafted to head that group. This decision was taken after a discussion between the Prime Minister, the Finance Minister and the Cabinet Secretary. Hence, there was no choice. Had I been given a choice, I would have loved to continue to serve the poorest of the poor for this additional year but I was now assigned the task of serving the richest of the rich.

As I got out of the room, there was a buzz on my phone. One of my school friends who had risen to become the chairman of a public sector bank called me. He informed me that the Finance Minister had just announced in a meeting of bankers in Mumbai that a 'Swarup Panel' had been constituted to fast-track projects that had an investment of INR 1000 crores or more.

The government had for once demonstrated that they could act fast if they so desired. For me, it was yet another journey in an uncharted territory at a time when scams were breaking out each day and I was to facilitate clearance of high value projects.

Unwanted ... at least in the beginning

No one except the Finance Minister wanted the projects to be fast-tracked. They could not be blamed. The atmosphere had been vitiated. If you did not do anything, then nothing would happen to you. However, if you did something, then anything could happen. Everyone was concerned about saving his own back. There was no concern about the damage to the economy as a whole. However, what surprised me most was the attitude of those that should have been concerned about the impact of such delays. The tenor of discussions was appalling. The only concern was how not to make a mistake even if it meant not doing anything at all. The epithets used for entrepreneurs were disgusting. Those that were apparently assisting the Finance Minister in putting in place the institution of the Project Monitoring Group (PMG), used these epithets. The Department of Economic Affairs was surprisingly indifferent to what was being attempted in the PMG and the Department of Financial Services (responsible for the banking sector). They made all possible efforts to keep it at as safe a distance as possible.

There was initial reservation even amongst those ministries that were actually to benefit from the resolution of such issues. This happened primarily because of the lack of ownership of projects even though the objectives of the ministries were to be served through rapid implementation. For example, it took me some effort to convince the representative of the Power Ministry to sponsor private sector power projects that were stuck because of delay in clearances. The ministry finally came on board and promoted such projects quite aggressively. The same could not be said of a number of other ministries that took a long time to fathom the utility of the new mechanism that was put in place.

The ministries that had created problems and caused delays were obviously apprehensive about the new institution. No one wanted to be 'told' anything or 'pushed' to do anything. One of the secretaries even wrote a nasty letter reminding the PMG that if the projects were fast tracked they would attract the attention of the Central Bureau of Investigation (CBI) and the courts. The letter was endorsed by several persons and conveniently found its way into the media, creating a lot of embarrassment for everyone. However, over a period, this very ministry discovered the utility of the PMG and started using the platform for resolution of issues that were of concern to them. The other 'recipient' (the term 'recipient' was a euphemism for such ministries that were apparently sitting on clearances) ministries also came around but gradually and grudgingly. The weekly meetings rattled them from a stupor. The consistent persistence of the PMG was annoying. Initially no one was prepared to concede an inch. In fact, in one of the meetings, the representative of the Department of Financial Services clearly stated that they could not issue any directive to the banks.

There was an initial reluctance on the part of the states. The instrumentality of the PMG was perceived as impinging on their authority. Traditionally, any issue relating to the state government was considered in meetings held in Delhi where the state officials were invited. The PMG altered this and started travelling to the states to discuss with the state officials. The central team visiting the states invited apprehension, though these apprehensions were soon dispelled. The states not only started welcoming the central team, quite a few of them set up their own mechanism to fast-track clearances.

The industry was dispirited, dejected and frustrated. They were not sure how the new institution of the PMG would evolve. The 'consultants' speaking on behalf of the industry were always critical of what was happening. 'Decision Paralysis' was the criticism levelled against the government. However, when decisions were taken, criticism shifted to non-implementation of decisions. When implementation was done well, questions were raised about the actual investment on the ground. Some of the questions raised were indeed relevant but there was a lot of cynicism that pervaded their utterances. In fact, one of the 'experts' who had served as a secretary general of an industry association and had failed to deliver something on the ground was at his critical and cynical best. He was indeed good at writing but had no clue about the nuances of implementation.

Surprisingly, the media was appreciative of the idea and a few positive stories were published.

The PMG ... gets going

Despite the initial cynicism and indifference, I moved on with it. The situation was grim, frustrating and dismal. It had been six months since the Cabinet Committee of Investment (CCI) had been set up to fast-track large-scale investment but it had not been able to make much of a headway, as there was no institution to do the legwork for this committee. The CCI met occasionally and few projects did come up for consideration. It was even more appalling that there was no mechanism to monitor and ensure the implementation of the decisions taken by the CCI. The media was critical of the lack of any development. A full-page news item in *The Economic Times* regarding the delays in clearance got everyone fuming. The PMG had just been born and already faced enormous challenges.

My designation was Head, Project Monitoring Group (PMG). However, there was no group in existence. In fact, there was no place to sit. I had to start from scratch. It turned out to be a blessing in disguise. There was no legacy. The edifice could be built based on the requirements of the stakeholders. The RSBY experience came handy in various ways. It was also built from the scratch. I had identified few worthy officers. Two of them were brought from the Ministry of Labour and Employment. These officers had worked with me and their commitment to tasks was exemplary. I chose the personal staff (very critical in any assignment) carefully and from among those who had worked with me earlier. Hence, the comfort and trust level was high. The team was completed with an outstanding officer, Dr V P Joy who joined as Joint Secretary.

To solve the problems of long pending clearances and approvals, it was felt the use of IT applications was necessary to bring transparency in the functioning of the PMG. This was not readily agreed to since in the Cabinet Secretariat almost all correspondence and papers were confidential. However, in due course, the need for conducting business in a transparent manner dawned on everyone. The technical team in the Cabinet Secretariat came handy. It put in place a web-based programme. Any industry proponent could create his own login and password and upload their cases pertaining to a specific ministry and/or state. Simultaneously, each ministry was asked to designate a joint-secretary level officer as the nodal officer. Once the project was accepted for consideration by the PMG, the project details and the issues relating to that ministry/department went automatically to the concerned nodal officers along with an automatic mailer. The nodal officer then had to provide comments on the portal itself. These comments were accessible to the concerned project proponent.

Subgroups were set up for each 'recepient' ministry (there were 12 of them till February 2014) and these subgroups met periodically on fixed days and time (three of them met every week). The project proponents made brief presentations on the issues that were discussed in the presence of representatives of the 'sponsoring ministry' and the 'recipient ministry'. The primary objective was to obtain a timeline for a decision to be taken by the recipient ministry. The minutes of the meeting were recorded on the portal at the time of the meeting itself. The discussions were focussed, and the meetings were short as quality groundwork was done by the respective ministries in advance.

Learning from the RSBY experience, the discussions were mostly held at the state headquarters and not in Delhi. This facilitated larger participation of the state bureaucracy, including the district collectors, and more in-depth and detailed deliberation on issues. This approach entailed a lot of travelling but it was well worth the effort as it facilitated marketing the concept behind the resolution of issues.

Industry associations like the Confederation of Indian Industries (CII) and the FICCI were leveraged to disseminate the message behind the setting up of PMG and the progress there under. Within a year, the PMG facilitated the resolution of issues pertaining to 156 projects entailing an investment of INR 5.60 lakh crore. The PMG had started showing results. The stakeholders were happy. The CII in its letter to the Prime Minister placed on record their 'appreciation for the good work being done by the PMG'. The FICCI felt that 'the model followed by PMG' could be 'replicated across the processes where approvals and clearances are granted under various departments'.

The PMG had started to roll and make things happen.

A 'tax' that could have been avoided

I received a call from the cabinet secretary, "Montek (Singh Ahluwalia) has desired that you should meet him". Montek, as he was popularly known, was the Deputy Chairman, Planning Commission. Again, the context of meeting was not revealed but I was summoned immediately. As I entered his room, he complimented me for the good work I was doing at the PMG. In reality, however, the delays in clearances pertaining to the Ministry of Environment and Forests were beginning to frustrate me. The crisis had reached epic proportions as a minister had been sitting on files relating to projects entailing investment of more than INR 50,000 crore. There were rumours that a 'tax' named after the Cabinet Minister was being charged. I myself had sent notes on three different occasions to the Cabinet Secretary requesting him to inform the Prime Minister about this specific case as such delays were likely to create embarrassment for the government that was already reeling under various scams.

When I conveyed my reservations in the current meeting, Montek asked for the details. I shared the problems that were being faced with the Ministry of Environment and Forests, and the potential fallout from it. He looked perplexed and enquired, "Have you informed the Prime Minister?" I told him that I had no access to the PM. He assured me, "OK, I will have a word with him". I returned to my room in the Vigyan Bhavan Annexe. In the late afternoon, there was a call from the Cabinet Secretary yet again. He had just had a long conversation with the PM. Normally an unflappable person, he appeared a trifle perturbed.

"What did you tell Montek?" he questioned.

"I told him all that I have been telling you for the past couple of months," was my response. "Everything?" he was surprised and then regaining his composure, "No wonder the PM wanted to know more about it".

It was evident that Montek had spoken to the PM. The Principal Secretary to the PM rang me up the next day and sought further details. Those could be sent promptly, as a soft copy of everything was available on the website. He was not only surprised at the speed with which I had managed to furnish the details but also at the availability of the soft files. The details disclosed that files and decisions were being held up in the Ministry of Environment and Forests.

Nothing happened during the next one week. I had a chance meeting with Oscar Fernandez (with whom I had worked when he was the Labour Minister) in that period. He had subsequently been moved to another ministry. As both of us had arrived ahead of the scheduled time at the conference, we started chatting. I used this opportunity to broach the issue related to delays in clearance by the Ministry of Environment and Forests and the associated rumours regarding 'speed money' that infamously came to be known by the name of a cabinet minister. It was rumoured that this money was being collected for the party fund. Oscar Fernandez had heard similar rumours. Being close to the 'family', I suggested that as the name was dragged into this mess, he should inform the 'high command'. I don't know what happened after this to trigger the decision but the concerned minister was shown the door, within a week.

Transparency had apparently claimed its first victim.

The Coal Conundrum

Hitting the ground running

It was early morning when I noticed the SMS and the batchmate who had sent it was not prone to sending frivolous messages. She was also not an early riser. The message read—"Congratulations". Within minutes, a similar message popped up on my Facebook wall. I wasn't sure what I had done to deserve this. It was middle of the month and normally transfers or promotions were announced during the last few days of each month. I accessed the Department of Personnel and Training website out of curiosity and there it was—I was posted as Officer on Special Duty in the rank of Secretary in the Ministry of Coal. The post was created to accommodate me in the ministry a fortnight before my formal takeover as Secretary on the retirement of the existing incumbent.

I was keen on continuing with the PMG for some more time, as there were some tasks still to be accomplished to ensure fast-tracking of projects. There was a need for setting up a web-based system for getting all the clearances and I was working towards it. Anyway, the government had felt otherwise. There was a crisis to be managed and I was chosen to manage this crisis. What I discovered subsequently, 'crisis' would be an understatement for that.

A large number of friends and well-wishers sympathised with me as I was selected to occupy the 'hot' seat. I was not fully conversant with the functioning of the Coal Ministry, so I asked a colleague for details. He replied, "Have you seen 'Gangs of Wasseypur'?" This was a hard-hitting movie on coal mafia. His response made it all clear.

I joined the Coal Ministry on 16 October. On the very next day, in a meeting presided over by the PM, a presentation was made wherein all the woes of the power sector were attributed to the problems with coal. There was indeed a crisis because of coal shortage, but I could not swallow the argument that coal was the only cause for the pathetic state of affairs in the power sector. Despite being new to the job, I pointed out that the power sector required a more comprehensive look. The PM agreed with me but still went on to state that if I could resolve coal-related issues, the economy would thrive. (Coal issues got substantially resolved eventually, but it is debatable if the economy thrived as a consequence!) There was also a message to finalise an ordinance to take care of the situation created by the Supreme Court order cancelling allocation of 204 coal blocks. The ordinance was to be presented to the cabinet on 20 October. That was only 72 hours away. It was a stupendous task but was successfully accomplished by a committed team of officers.

I hit the ground running.

"Is that so, Mr Swarup?"

In view of the urgency to bring about a legislation to tackle the situation created as a consequence of the Supreme Court judgement, an ordinance was promulgated. However, the real challenge was to get the related bill passed by the parliament. It was easy to get the bill introduced and cleared in the Lok Sabha, but the real test was to get it past the Rajya Sabha where the government did not have the majority. Moreover, the opposition parties were in no mood to play ball. They were keen to pay the government in the same coin by repeatedly disrupting the functioning of the parliament. Precious time was being lost. However, they could not care less. Consequently, in the absence of legislative business, most of the bills that were introduced in the parliament were languishing.

To carry out the auction of the coal blocks that were cancelled by the Supreme Court, it was imperative to get the aforementioned legislation passed. Hence, a multipronged strategy was chalked out to reach out to the parliamentarians and those that mattered and to convey the value proposition behind the legislation.

One of the parts of the strategy was to reach out to the chief ministers of the opposition-ruled states (states where non-NDA parties were in power). On one of the rare holidays, I was with my family as we drove down to a friend's place in Gurgaon. I got a message from Mr Arun Jaitley's house that the Chief Minister of Odisha Mr Naveen Patnaik had arrived at his residence and Mr Jaitley would like to invite me to come over and explain the proposed legislation to him. I beat a retreat and reached Mr Jaitley's residence. I was ushered into a room where Mr Jaitley, Mr Naveen Patnaik, CM, Odisha, Mr Piyush Goyal, Minister of State (Independent Charge) for Power and Coal and the Personal Secretary to the CM, Odisha were already present. Mr Goyal was explaining something to the CM as I walked in. Mr Jaitley interrupted him and introduced me to the CM. I was then asked to explain the bill and its rationale. I made an opening statement keeping in mind that the CM was upset at his state getting a smaller amount from the auctions as compared to Chhattisgarh. I explained that the central government was not getting a single penny out of these auctions, yet it was putting in all the effort to auction the blocks in a transparent manner. He was surprised and it showed in his response, “Is that so, Mr Swarup?” Then I went on to explain the full process of auction. My statements and explanations were interspersed with his, “Is that so, Mr Swarup!” on a few occasions. I used my smartphone and went to the web portal where the live auction was being webcast. Fortunately, an Odisha based mine was being auctioned. I explained that every INR 2 increase in the bid translated into INR 50 lakhs for the state. He could not but be impressed with the way the auctions were being conducted. Finally, what clinched the issue was my statement that the state of Odisha would get around INR 27,000 crores through these auctions. This was the last “Is that so, Mr Swarup!” Biju Janata Dal (BJD) supported the Bill in the Parliament.

The Rai Sahebs

There is no dearth of advisors in India. They are all around you. These 'Rai Sahebs' (advisors) come in all shapes and sizes. Some have the sophisticated presence and appearance like McKinsey & Company, KPMG and PWC, a number of them are retired government officials (not all of whom did anything worthy of note as serving officers) and some are self-professed and well-connected experts. Quite a few of them do not even charge you for the advice so long as you allow them to sneak into your domain which they believe is theirs.

Consequent to the cancellation of the coal blocks by the Supreme Court, the new government wanted to set in motion a process to auction the coal blocks. I had been drafted to carry out this task as Secretary of the Ministry. However, not everyone was convinced that the process being evolved for the auction of coal blocks would withstand scrutiny and the expectations associated with it. It was too sensitive a matter to be left just to the mandarins of the Coal Ministry. The people incharge perhaps trusted the bureaucracy but did not have enough confidence in them to allow a free hand. Hence, an informal proposal was mooted for a committee under Mr Vinod Rai, who had been responsible for pointing out the irregularity in the allocation of coal blocks in his role as Comptroller and Auditor General. It was hoped that he would give 'rai' to the Coal Ministry in the conduct of coal block auctions, although he was not keen on giving any 'rai' on his own.

The atmosphere was charged. Discussions were held in the room of the Principal Secretary in the PMO. He had suggested that there should be a committee to oversee coal block auctions. I opposed it. As Secretary of the Ministry, I was not willing to have any such committee breathing down my neck in the form of supervision. I was clear that the task of carrying out the auction was ours. Hence, we were prepared to take all the responsibility associated with it. There was a heated debate as I continued to resist. Normally no one argued with the PMO. The PMO was the final arbiter in all sensitive issues. Everyone was heard but the final 'hint' came from this office. In this case, it was the Principal Secretary himself. However, even with the risk of being impertinent, I stuck to my guns. I was clear that if I was in charge, I would lead the way. I was not opposed to seeking advice or consulting those around. But, there was no way in which a formal consultative, supervisory or advisory committee was acceptable to me. Having worked with me in the past, he perhaps knew that I would not relent easily. After a lot of fireworks, bordering on unpleasantness, the idea was shelved. We were spared the structured consultation of the 'Rai Sahebs' though we continued to be benefitted by informal advice right through the process of auctions.

Coal block auctions ... from darkness to light

There was a crisis at hand. The coal blocks that had been allotted during the past decade and a half came under the scanner. The Supreme Court cancelled all 204 blocks that had been allocated since 1993 terming such allocations 'arbitrary'. India has the third largest reserves of coal and yet the coal production in the country, despite huge reserves, was lagging behind the demand. The decision of the Supreme Court implied that if necessary corrective steps were not taken immediately, the production of coal would suffer further.

The Supreme Court through its judgements came down heavily on the 'non-transparent' and discretionary allocation of coal blocks that had resulted in a windfall for the private sector and loss to the public exchequer. In its orders dated 25 August and 24 September 2014, it cancelled the coal block allocations. In its decision, the response court also ordered that such 42 coal blocks where mining was being done would cease to mine after 31 March 2015.

The government had to act and quickly. The time available for putting in place alternative lessees to carry on mining in 42 blocks (with a peak rate capacity of 90 million tons) was only a few months (up to 31 March 2015). The legislation had to be passed to carry out the onerous task. The parliament was not in session. Hence, an ordinance was promulgated. The ordinance sought to plug the 'legislative gap' and put in place a legal framework to manage the crisis. One of the primary objectives here was to ensure that the coal production did not suffer as a consequence of the cancellation of coal blocks. This was sought to be achieved through a transparent and expeditious allocation of coal blocks.

A transparent auction process was put in place. It was not an easy task as it was unprecedented. There was a time constraint as well as entities had to be found to carry on mining in such 42 mines where mining was already underway. The 'past' of the Coal Ministry and the atmosphere of 'distrust' made the task difficult as there was reluctance at various levels to commit on files. To make matters worse, the stakes were extremely high. Almost anyone who was someone had a stake in the process. Finally, everyone was busy monitoring what was going on. Everyone wanted results, quickly. However, few had any clue about how it would be done. A crack team was constituted, and after some debate, a joint secretary level officer was appointed as nominated authority. This too was not easy as there was a debate about whether a judicial officer or an administrative officer should be appointed. Finally, Vivek Bhardwaj, an IAS officer in the ministry was given the charge. Much of the credit for the success of the coal block auctions should go to this officer for his clear understanding of issues, his out-of-the-box thinking, meticulous planning and for getting all the stakeholders on board. SBI Caps was engaged to finalise various documents and to assist in evaluating bids. Metal Scrap Trading Corporation (MSTC) created the electronic platform for bidding.

A two-stage online electronic auction process was put in place. The entire database of coal mines (including Geological Reports) was made available in electronic format to the bidders. The bidders could bid only for such mines whose documents they purchased online. There were other eligibility criteria for the bidder to bid.

To ensure that the auction process did not lead to an increase in power tariff, a 'reverse auction' mechanism was devised for the 'regulated' (power) sector. In this case, the rate quoted by successful bidder determined its variable charge. Ascending (or forward) auction was adopted for non- regulated sector. Here, the objective was to optimise revenues.

In the first stage of the auction, an initial price offer (IPO) was to be submitted along with the technical bid, on the MSTC e-auction platform in encrypted form. The IPOs from only technically qualified bidders were opened. The qualified bidders were placed in descending/ascending order (as the case may be). Only the top 50% amongst these IPOs ('qualified bidder') were allowed to participate in the e-auction.

For the e-auction, the new floor/ceiling price was the highest/lowest IPO received from the technically qualified bidders. The initial e-auction window was for 2 hours with the auto-extending option of 8 minutes each till bids ceased within that period.

Transparency was key in these auctions. All technical bids were opened in the presence of the bidder and displayed on-screen. Auction proceedings were webcast live.

The successful auction and allotment not only met the requirements of the end-use sectors viz. iron and steel, cement and power including Captive Power Plant (CPP), but also had the potential of generating a significant amount of revenue for the concerned state governments through e-auction proceeds, royalty and upfront payment.

It was a classic example of 'cooperative federalism' where all the revenues and benefits accrue to the states or the consumers and none to the central government. Intensive interactions were held with all the concerned state governments to keep them on board. It helped to convert the ordinance into legislation subsequently even at a time when some of the states were opposed to the central government on several other issues.

The coal block auctions clearly demonstrated that the transparent use of IT applications could help in realising/determining 'fair' value of natural resources. Outsourcing activities to expert bodies like SBI Caps and MSTC contributed substantially to the success of the auctions. What made a difference was taking the stakeholders on board. It enabled us to fast-track various processes. The group made a lot of mistakes as it went along. However, there was a candid admission of such mistakes and corrections were made. Finally, what really mattered was 'walking the walk'.

The real coal story

Many thought, and still think, that the smooth auction of coal blocks was 'the coal story'. It was not. The process of coal blocks auctions was primarily to put in place a transparent mechanism to distribute a natural resource that was so critical. In fact, the real problem in the country was a shortage of coal and the coal block auctions had a minor impact on the coal production.

India sits on an estimated reserve of 300 billion tons of coal. Yet the country is short of coal. Consequent to the opening of the power sector in 2004, the demand for coal suddenly shot up. Import of 21.7 million tons in 2006 grew to 131.3 million tons in 2014. The gap between demand and supply that was minimal at the beginning of this millennium, grew substantially.

DOMESTIC DEMAND AND SUPPLY (In MTE)

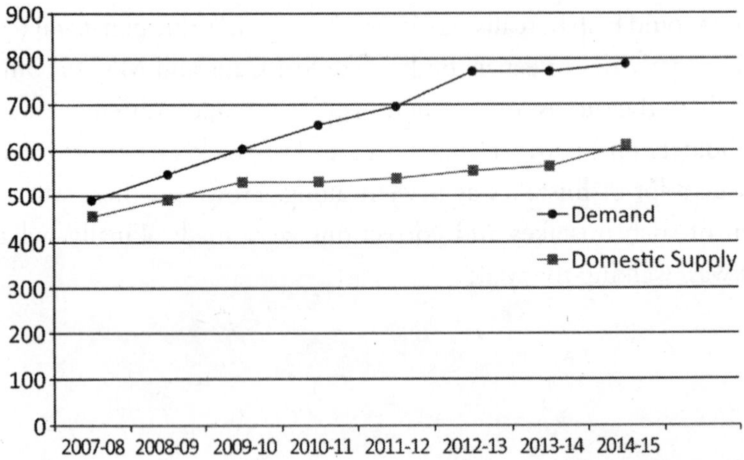

(Source: Annual Plan, Ministry of Coal)

The so-called 'coal scam' emerged out of this scarcity when there was a scramble for coal blocks.

When I took over as Coal Secretary, the focus was obviously on the coal block auctions in the beginning. However, one could soon discern the root cause of the acute shortage of coal. A quick analysis revealed that the following factors were critical to coal production in the country.

1. Land acquisition
2. Environment and Forest clearances
3. Availability of railway rakes to transport coal

Land acquisition was becoming increasingly tough because of the politics that had crept into the entire process. The extant legislation had brought everything to a grinding halt in most of the sectors, including coal even though land acquisition for coal mining was governed by Coal Bearing Areas (Acquisition and Development) Act, 1957. The process was by and large in the hands of the state governments that were at best indifferent, unable to gauge the opportunity size.

Geologically most of the coal reserves were in forest areas. Environment and Forests clearances entailed a lengthy process involving various levels of bureaucracy. Most of the processing had to be done by state-level functionaries before it came to the centre for the final clearance.

No matter how much coal was produced, it would be of no consequence if it was not transported to the user industry. Most of these user industries, including power plants, were at a substantial distance from pitheads. Transportation of coal by railways was not only economical but also environment-friendly. All the coal mines were not connected with railheads and where they were, there was a perennial shortage of rakes. There were competing demands on these rakes from food and steel sectors.

Some steps were taken to take care of these problems—

1. Using the experience of the Project Monitoring Group, a web-based Project Monitoring Portal was set up to monitor and pursue various clearances. The information on the portal was updated in real time.

2. An institutional arrangement was made to hold meetings every month on a fixed date and time with the officers of the Ministry of Railways and the Ministry of Environment and Forests.
3. Instead of holding meetings with the states at Delhi to resolve state-level issues, regular visits were made to the states. This provided an opportunity to interact with a considerable number of field functionaries who were directly involved in the processing of an application for clearances. It turned out to be a game changer as it enabled us to convey a value proposition to the states. Excavation of coal resulted in an enormous amount of revenue to the states by way of taxes as well as direct and indirect employment generation.
4. Plan for ramping up of coal production in consultation with the stakeholders brought greater ownership of the decision taken later based on such plans.

The impact of the following steps was unprecedented—

1. More than 5500 hectares of land was acquired by Coal India Limited (CIL) during the year 2014-15. This was the highest ever acquisition in the past few years. This acquisition happened when all other organisations were struggling to acquire even a few hectares.
2. Environment and Forests clearances were obtained for more than 3400 hectares.
3. Against the availability of 194 railway rakes available during 2014-15 (which in itself was a record), 213 rakes were made available during 2015-16. Both railways and coal sectors benefitted out of this arrangement.

The resolution of these issues led to an unprecedented incremental growth of 32 million tons in coal production during the year 2014-15. This was more than the cumulative incremental growth of 31 million tons during the preceding four years. The cumulative incremental production of 74 million tons during 2014-15 and 2015-16 was equivalent to the incremental production during the entire 11th Plan.

PRODUCTION OF CIL (In MTE)

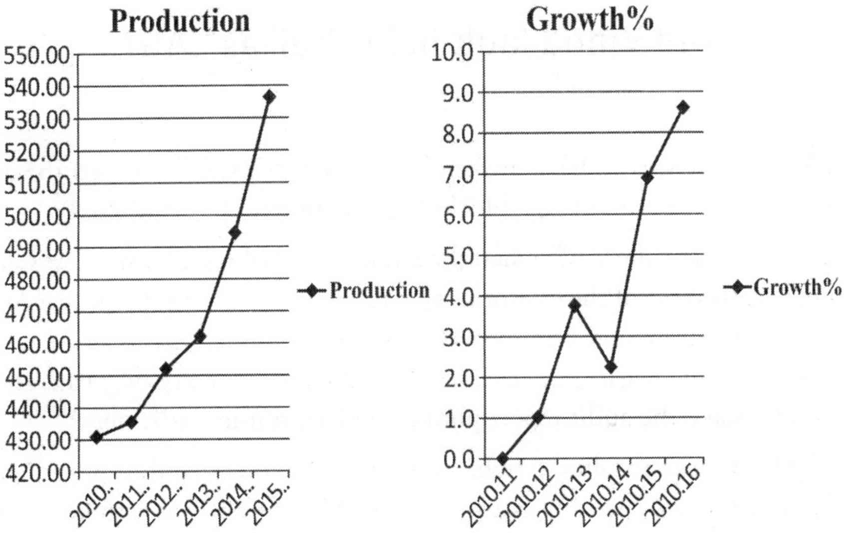

Consequent to this increase in the production of coal, the thermal power plants had an average inventory of coal for more than 20 days. Central Electricity Authority deemed no plant critical in terms of shortage of coal. Import of coal came down substantially during 2015-16 resulting in a foreign exchange saving of more than INR 24,000 crore.

The Economic Times termed it a 'dramatic turnaround'.

Did Vinod fault in his 'rai' as CAG?

All hell seemed to have broken loose when the CAG released the audit report on the allocation of coal blocks made between 2004 and 2010.

Vinod Rai was the CAG when the audit of coal block allocation was done. Responding to some of the questions against the report, in his book *Not Just an Accountant*, he has raised certain pertinent questions—"What was the CAG's folly in this entire saga? The decision to audit the Ministry of Coal? Or the decision to make the audit report public by placing it in Parliament?"

The CAG was absolutely right on both these counts and in pointing out the flaws in the process of allocation of coal blocks that was termed as 'non-transparent' and 'discretionary'. However, was the CAG wrong in determining the loss to the public exchequer? Was there a need to make a public spectacle of what he thought was right? Did this create an environment where decision-making became even more difficult? These are some of the questions that should have been raised but were neither raised nor answered. Almost everyone was blinded by the enormity of the issues that came to the fore but were blissfully oblivious of the implications of stretching and highlighting the issues in the way it was done.

In the book, data from the CAG report was used and the calculations were worked out as follows:

(a) Average CIL selling price: INR 1028/Ton

(b) The average cost of coal mining: INR 583/Ton

(c) Financing cost: INR 150/Ton

(d) Financial Benefit {a-(b+c)}: INR 295/Ton

(e) Extractable Reserves: 6282 MT

(f) Financial Gain {dxe}: INR 1,80,000 cr

Let us look at each one of these aspects. The cost of coal mining by CIL ranges between INR 400 and INR 4000 per ton. Given this wide range, arriving at an average cost of mining, as was done by the CAG, was most inappropriate. In fact, the cost of mining varies significantly from one mine to the other because of several factors. There are issues relating to stripping ratio, grade of coal and transportation cost that were totally ignored by the CAG in arriving at the correct numbers. There was another aspect to it as well. Apart from the cost of mining, the then Coal Secretary had conceded before the Parliamentary Committee that there was a stark difference in the quality of coal in the blocks with the CIL and those given to private parties for captive mining. Hence, the use of CIL numbers as benchmarks was faulty. If one looks at the statistics provided by the Coal Controller of India for the year 2014-15, it is evident that while 33.20% of the coal mined by CIL was of superior quality (Grades 1 to 9), only 9.4% of the coal mined by captive miners was of that grade. Similarly, the stripping ratio for captive mines was much higher than the one for CIL mines. During the year 2013-14, it was 1.89 for CIL and 3.46 in the captive blocks.

Such a calculation led to the cancellation of even those mines for which there are no takers even now. A careful calculation (if at all) would have clearly determined the 'windfall' gain from each mine. However, in a rush to give a report, average numbers were used. If mine-wise analysis, based on facts, had been made, allocation of only those mines would have been cancelled where there was a windfall gain. Consequent to the CAG report, allocation of even underground mines (where the cost of mining was remarkably high) was also cancelled. Ironically, as mentioned earlier, there are no takers of such mines even today. There were indeed some mines where there were huge margins and the allocation of such mines deserved to be cancelled but we ended up dumping all the allocations lock, stock and barrel.

The next logical question would be, if margins were not so high, how did the government manage to garner an estimated amount of INR 1.96 lakh crores by way of an auction of only 31 mines that were auctioned in 2015? We must look at the context of the auctions. The bidding in the auction was decided by the following factors—

1. Perceived (actual) shortage of coal in the country
2. Uncertainty about imported coal price and availability

3. Committed expenditure in fixed assets like power/steel plants that were ready for production, but the allocated blocks were cancelled.
4. Uncertainty about the future availability of coal blocks.

All the above factors led to 'irrational bidding' for most of the blocks. The following points support this:

(a) The auctioned blocks were supposed to have produced 56 million tons. But, on an average, they are producing only 16 million tons per annum so far. In fact, a number of blocks haven't even started production.

(b) Some allottees went to the court with a view to somehow wriggle out of the hole they had gotten themselves into.

Ironically for 9 blocks put on auction during the 4th round in 2016, there were hardly any takers. No auction took place thereafter though there are still 120 blocks. If the CAG's calculations were extrapolated, then there would still be around INR 3.13 lakh crore tied up in these blocks. If there was a margin of INR 295 per ton, then why were there no takers?

What the CAG could not visualise was the impact of Coal India production on the price of coal available in India. As the production of coal increased, and as the availability improved, the auction price of Coal India came down substantially. This affected the desire of the entrepreneurs to go for coal blocks. The so-called margin of INR 295 as determined by the CAG was not available. As argued earlier, it is a debatable point whether such a margin was ever available on every block. By clubbing all the blocks together in deciding the 'right' and the 'wrong', enormous damage was done. The fact that some of the blocks were auctioned for more than INR 295 per ton does not justify the determination of 'windfall' for all the blocks. Like a true auditor (and not an accountant), details should have been worked out for each block. Averages do not work in such situations.

Vinod Rai states in his book that all the records showed was that the Committee met, deliberated and merely recorded the name of the block allotted to a company, and the state where the end-use plant existed. He finds fault with this. As an ex-civil servant, he should know that that is how the minutes are recorded, especially when there is a consensus. It is only when there is a difference of opinion that such an opinion and the reasons for overruling it are recorded. The CAG, it appeared, was on a fault-finding mission. Hence, apart from finding fault where it did exist, he also found fault where it did not.

The job of any civil servant, more so of the CAG, is to do his job quietly and not go to town (though this is changing fast). Gauging the mood of the country, the CAG report was 'launched' at a press conference. The image of the Deputy CAG flashing the report before the media is etched in everyone's memory. Yes, a wrong had been committed. Yes, it is the job of the CAG to detect these 'wrongs'. Yes, it is also the job of CAG to inform the parliament about the wrongs. However, perhaps making a public spectacle of the report was not becoming of a civil servant. In his book *Not Just an Accountant*, Vinod Rai justifies going to the media. He was right in doing so. However, he played to the gallery in the way the press meet was organised by the CAG. He has set a precedent where future CAGs may also want to become Vinod Rais. His immediate successor did try to become one but met with stiff resistance from a much stronger government.

Had the CAG taken care to go into the details of each mine and had he not taken the 'half-truth' to town, the consequences on the decision-making process would not have been so devastating. Bureaucratic decision-making suffered enormously. It is debatable whether the high profiling of the report by the CAG was essential to correct the system. It would be too much to credit the CAG for the transparency that came about in the later auctions of the coal blocks. Transparency was made possible by the commitment of the new government. Transparency was built in areas where the CAG had no role to play whatsoever.

In his book *The Coal Conundrum*, Mr P C Parakh has been kind to the CAG—"It was not necessary for the CAG to arrive at mathematically acceptable figures for establishing its hypothesis". However, according to me, this was the problem. The CAG came up with numbers without going into the details. It was these numbers that created a 'Tsunami', got noticed and acted upon. Had it been a more precise mine-specific analysis, it would not have caused so much damage to the economy, bureaucratic 'psyche' and to honest civil servants like Mr Parakh himself who blames the judiciary but not the one who started it all.

Let us now look at the consequences of the CAG report:

1. Officers refrained from committing themselves on the files. They were playing 'safe'. It was evident during the examination of bids when the officers conducted the auctions subsequently. The concrete recommendations on the bids were initiated at the level of the secretary.
2. It was conjectured that the coal production would increase if the blocks were auctioned. This was not so. In fact, post-auction, the coal production from auctioned mines was well below the estimated amount. The coal situation in the country eased because of unprecedented increase of coal production by CIL that had nothing to do with the CAG or its report.
3. The CAG report led to the conviction of officers that enjoyed a spotless image. The then Prime Minister who in his role as Coal Minister had approved the proposals to allocate coal blocks conveniently dissociated himself from the process. The CAG obviously cannot be blamed for all of this, but he set the tone for devastating consequences.

Storm in a teacup creates a tsunami

"Why to blame only *netas*, 5Cs also hinder decision making" : Coal Secretary.

This was the headline of a leading daily that generated a tsunami of reactions. Perhaps almost everyone felt it, but no one had the courage to state it. It all began with a small comment made on Facebook and Twitter:

"Pace of development is not so much impacted by the dishonest as by inhibiting factors that prevent the honest from taking decisions".

This came from the depth of my heart and this went viral on the net though it was still a storm in the teacup. However, the subsequent explanation on Facebook created a tsunami as it impacted the holy cows of governance in the country:

"We very conveniently blame politicians for all the ills. However, isn't it true that 5 Cs (namely CBI, CVC, CAG, CIC and Courts) contribute substantially to create an inhibiting environment for quick and effective decision making that impact development? Ironically all these institutions are not occupied by politicians but by civil servants".

There was a deluge of reactions, almost all of it in support of the aforementioned statement. An ex-cabinet secretary remarked, "Anil Swarup is spot on. To make matters worse the C's have begun playing more and more to the gallery in the last few years". A secretary, known to be close to the powers, commented, "You have made a very bold statement on FB. Kudos!" Another secretary was equally forthright, "A truly bold statement, Anil. Cheers! You are changing the images of 'bureaucrat'". An ex-ambassador to the WTO quipped, "Well done, Anil. You have hit the nail squarely on the head". A retired IPS officer who had worked with the CBI agreed with the statement, "With my fairly long experience of CBI, I fully endorse the view of Anil". Another IPS officer, heading a central paramilitary force, also commented, "He's correct ... We have often discussed this point. Ours is the only country where the aforesaid entities, rightly called commentators, are considered more important than players! Or, put differently, conductors of post-mortem more important than the doctor carrying out the diagnosis".

Interestingly, one of the Cs mentioned was the CAG. An Ex-DG, CAG went on to congratulate me for raising the issue, "Congratulations ... for raising pertinent issues hindering good and fast decisions in Government".

Some cabinet ministers rang me up to congratulate me for raising the issue.

I had flagged an issue appropriately while I was still in service. Some of the persons manning theses institutions had gone overboard to 'play to the gallery' killing initiative amongst those they left behind in the civil service and rendering decision making increasingly more difficult. No wonder governance has suffered and continues to suffer from the devastation caused by a CAG in the not-so-distant past and the likes of him. This was palpable in the Ministry of Coal where I now sought to construct something after the massive destruction caused by the demolishing squad.

Yearning to become famous

There is nothing wrong in becoming rich and famous. Many people have such an aspiration. This is also true of the civil servants. However, whereas becoming rich has cost a number of civil servants quite dearly, becoming famous has not. We have the likes of 'renowned' Election Commissioner who became famous not for what they did when they were civil servants but the 'lionesque' image they developed for themselves after they were safely ensconced in a constitutional post with no future thereafter. Hence, they could roar (something they did not do while in service) and become famous. However, the CAG who unveiled the 'coal scam' went a step further, he became famous by finding faults with others. He got an opportunity to do so and he made the best of this opportunity. His job could have been done quietly, but then he chose to become a hero. Indeed, he did become one and his 'findings' suited the opposition that subsequently became the proposition. As the Supreme Court put a stamp on what he did, no one has questioned what he did. What he stated created a tsunami that swept away the mightiest. Only posterity will finally determine the extent of truth in what he stated, but the syndrome that he left behind devastated decision making. His approach and findings became the most formidable deterrent to decision making. Moreover, enamoured by his 'success', his successor attempted to replicate such a 'success' as it was a straightforward way to becoming famous.

Taking advantage of the credibility that the CAG had built over the years, there were those that were busy arriving at conclusions based on half-truths and wrong interpretation of facts. They were on a mission to find faults, to flaunt them and become famous. There was no other reason that could explain such an approach.

The coal block auctions conducted because of the judgements of the Supreme Court in the months of August and September 2014 were hailed as transparent. There was all round satisfaction with the process that was put in place in record time. However, the fault-finding machinery of the CAG thought otherwise. The chief auditors were yet again on a fault finding mission.

The Manual of Orders for auditing by the CAG clearly stipulates that 'cases that are sub-judice or have been referred to arbitration will not be mentioned in such a way so as to prejudice the claim'. However, not only were comments made on matters that were sub-judice, the contentions and arguments used in a petition by a bidder were paraphrased and presented as audit observations. The CAG was requested to respond to a few queries. As the CAG refused to provide clarification on why a sub-judice matter was listed in its observation, the issue had to be referred to Attorney General who clearly opined that "comments/findings on sub-judice matters should not ordinarily form a part of the Report".

The CAG in its report made observations on the criteria adopted for re-examination and cancellation of coal mines and stated that to improve governance in this field there is a need to evolve broad guidelines which should be applied to all cases. The Attorney General went on to opine that "the absolute right to cancel the auction/tender process lay with the tendering authority. It was well settled that the right to refuse the lower or other tender was always available with the government. If the government were to frame such guidelines, it would undermine the absolute right to safeguard economic interests". (The stand of the government was subsequently vindicated as the courts too endorsed the approach on all the issues.)

Even the tenders floated by the CAG as an organisation gave the CAG the right to reject any tender without assigning any reason. Ironically, immediately after suggesting to the Ministry of Coal to evolve guidelines for the rejection of bids, the office of the CAG issued a Tender Notice on 27 July 2016 wherein it said it 'reserves the right to reject any or all the tenders received without assigning any reason'. Still, the CAG questioned the re-examination of some cases and the rejection of bids.

In the same draft, the CAG went a step further. The tender document had a condition that allowed only 50% of the technically qualified bidders to participate in the stage-II bidding. The CAG observed this would limit competition.

The aforementioned provision had been incorporated after a lot of deliberations and was based on a logical analysis of bidding behaviour. The fear of getting knocked out before the final auction forces the bidders not to have any tie-up inter se the bidders and to bid very aggressively at the initial price offered. This innovative provision resulted in securing the best value for the coal mines through fostering more competition. This issue was also raised in a Writ Petition. The Hon'ble High Court of Delhi in W.P. (C) No. 1384/2015 'M/s. Sharda Energy and Minerals Ltd. V/s Union of India' concluded that "the methodology adopted by the respondents was working well". The Attorney General had also given a clear opinion: "It is clear there is no illegality in the methodology/auction design adopted by the MoC". Despite a clear finding of the High Court, the CAG chose to question the process that had worked so well.

Audit failed to appreciate that in a market-driven auction mechanism where there was no information asymmetry and complete transparency, it was the market forces that determined the true value of an asset. Floor/Reserve prices were, therefore, only indicative and notional. The valuation of the coal mine was done strictly as per the methodology prescribed by the Cabinet Committee on Economic Affairs (CCEA) which was based on raw coal and not washed coal and notified price, not negotiated prices. Audit had chosen to disregard the judgement of the Delhi High Court in the matter of multiple bids by companies through joint ventures or subsidiaries.

Apart from glaring factual errors including a number of coal mines cancelled or selective quotes from CCEA decisions, it seemed that Audit had failed to even read the Act as it identified one company as a prior allottee where the Act had not done so. Even definitions given in the Act had not been considered. Part of the report echoed the writ petitions of some of the unsuccessful bidders in courts. Innovative features of the auction design like a two-stage financial bidding process or reverse bidding were neither fully understood nor appreciated by Audit.

On reading the draft report it was clear that the CAG had arrived at conclusions based on wrong facts, half facts and erroneous understanding of processes. The bias was also evident in the way the entire process of audit was managed. The auction process was completed in less than 90 days. The audit took more than 7 months. The revised draft audit report was forwarded on 26 February and sought comments on the report containing 98 pages, 9 chapters and innumerable observations latest by 11 March 2016, i.e., within two weeks. It was also mentioned that in case no comments were received they would be forced to go ahead with the draft report. These queries required a detailed response from the ministry. The first draft audit report was forwarded to the ministry on 8 January 2016. All the urgency was displayed evidently for submitting the report during the budget session of the parliament perhaps with a view to extracting maximum mileage. However, as is apparent, gross misdemeanours were not actually misdemeanours at all and were backed by the opinion of the highest law officer of the land; the initial findings of the audit did not take off.

Someone was indeed trying to become famous. However, on this occasion, it was not to be. On this occasion, the CAG was up against a more determined government that was in no mood to take such frivolous allegations lying down. The averments in the draft report were contested with the backing of the comments of the Attorney General. The CAG had to back down substantially in its final report.

The Blinding Arc Lights of School Education

When I heard about my shifting from the dark dungeons of coal mines to the bright lights of school education, it was bliss. It was a journey from darkness to light. My post was Secretary, School Education and Literacy. Soon, I discovered that whereas in the coal sector, mining was underground and mafias operated above, in the 'mine' of school education it was the other way round. All the mafias existed underground, and they were all masked, masquerading as 'noble giants'. Having taken on some of the mafias of the coal sector and being partly successful in bringing the coal sector to order, the task now was to handle these 'noble giants'. It was made more difficult as there was no public outrage against invisible scams in education as there had been in the case of coal. Everything was seemingly in order. To make matters worse, I was the fifth person to hold the charge of Secretary in the past two and half years. Most of my predecessors had impeccable credentials in the education sector but either they did not continue or were not allowed to continue. The government apparently found in me the most 'uneducated' person (I had never worked in this sector except for a brief tenure of 3 months in Adult Education in the state of UP) to handle this sector.

It would be an understatement to say that the education sector was in bad shape. Yes, all the investments made by the government, especially those under mid-day meal, had resulted in children coming to school. But, as Minister Prakash Javadekar often said, it merely resulted in *aana-khaana-jaana* (coming-eating-going) with very little education being imparted. There had been a decline in the enrolment in government schools from 72.9% in 2007 to 63.1% in 2014. The Right to Children to Free and Compulsory Education Act 2009 (RTE Act) did little to stem the rot. The number of teachers in primary schools saw a jump from 31.82 lakhs in 98-99 to 46.84 lakhs in 2014-15 improving the student-teacher ratio from 42:1 to 24:1 in primary schools. However, all this made a negligible impact in terms of learning outcomes. Evaluations had revealed that the situation in terms of learning had become worse. There was a decline in the number of children in standard-V who could read a textbook of standard-II. The figure went down from 56.7% in 2007 to 42.2% in 2014. In Maths, it was worse. The percentage of children in standard-V who could divide came down from 41.0% to 20.7%. The budgetary allocation for school education was INR 55,115 crores during 2014-15. As a percentage of GDP, it was 0.52% and 3.07% of the entire budget. This amount was reduced further during subsequent years. Even during 2016-17, the allocated amount of INR 43,554 Crore was less than the allocation made for 2014-15. As a percentage of the GDP, it came down to 0.36% and 2.16% of the budget.

On the human resource front too, the situation was alarming. The department had had five secretaries between 2014 and 2016. A number of Joint Secretaries were also changed during this period. It was like musical chairs reminiscent of my days in UP where it was rumoured that the only industry flourishing was the transfer industry.

In the two biggest states of the country, the positioning of top management followed a peculiar pattern. Whereas in UP there were two additional chief secretary level officers manning school education and secondary education separately (creating huge coordination problems), in the state of Bihar, one officer looked after both Education and Health Departments. Consequently, the health of education continued to suffer.

There was a huge crisis. It was challenging to light up the coal sector, but it soon became evident that the education sector would require greater indulgence. The good news, however, was that I had a wonderful team.

A farce called 'moderation'

It indeed was a collusive yet competitive farce that was being perpetrated by a number of state education boards and the Central Board of Secondary Education (CBSE) in the name of 'moderation'. Broadly speaking, a child who got 16% marks in a particular subject could pass with grace marks (around 5%) and across the board the jacking up of marks was around 10%. Thus, we had a scenario where students who should have been detained, by a long margin, passed. There was another problem. Almost every student got 10% marks more than what he actually deserved. This led to a situation where a large number of students scored 95% in CBSE as this was the ceiling of 'spiking' set by CBSE. Effectively every student who got marks between 85% and 95% ended up getting 95%. What could be a greater farce! In some other boards, the ceiling was as high as 100%. This resulted in students getting 100% even in subjects like English. Shakespeare would indeed be turning in his grave. The situation was not considered grave enough in India as the 'present' was benefiting at the cost of the future.

Despite this farce, the all India pass percentage of 80% in CBSE was a poor reflection of our education system. The pass percentage would have plummeted substantially had this inflation of marks been disallowed. No one was prepared to face facts. The chairman of a state board who chose to face the facts and disallowed gracious dispensation was sacked.

The moderation policy of CBSE centred on the following tenets:

1. To compensate the candidates for the difficulties experienced in solving the question in a specified time due to misinterpretation/ambiguity of questions and errors, if any, leading to a multiplicity of performance and causing constraints on consumption of time for other questions.
2. To compensate for the vagaries and to bring uniformity in the evaluation process.

3. To bring parity on account of element of subjectivity involved in the evaluation.
4. To level up the mean achievements in the set-wise performance of the candidates attributable to the difference in the difficulty level of different sets of question papers in the multiple sets scheme.
5. To maintain a near parity of pass percentage of the candidates in the current year vis-à-vis preceding years, subject wise and overall.
6. To safeguard against arbitrary and careless evaluation due to the variance in the competency of examiners.

The giveaway was point 5 that indicated 'to maintain a near parity of pass percentage of the candidates in the current year vis-à-vis preceding years, subject wise overall'. This farcical pass percentage was allowed to continue because of this provision. Mistake once committed was mandated to be perpetuated.

When I took over as Secretary, School Education and Literacy, the Union Minister for Human Resource Development expressed concern over the issue during my initial meetings with them. Hence, I evolved a strategy to take care of this malaise. During my visits to the states and union territories (21 in the initial few months), the issue was discussed with the concerned authorities. Almost everyone agreed that this pernicious practice should be stopped but they were compelled to continue as others would not stop. Having got the views of most of the states, I decided to convene a national meet to discuss the issue. Quite surprisingly a consensus was arrived at. Based on the discussions and the consensus, the following decisions were recorded in the meeting held on 24 April 2017.

(a) All the state boards, except Kerala, decided to stop awarding moderation of marks for upward revision/spiking of marks from the current year and subject to amendment in the state regulations if required. However, the Kerala board confirmed it would to do away with moderation from the next year.

(b) They decided to continue with the policy of grace marks for low-level performance to improve the pass percentage, but the policy would be placed on the board's website for transparency. It was also decided that grace marks would be shown distinctly in the marksheet.

(c) They decided to move progressively towards adopting Common Core Curriculum in all major subjects up to class XII with the option to contextualise the contents in social science.

(d) They further decided to reflect marks/ grades for extracurricular activities separately in the marksheet.

(e) It was decided that the state boards may use National Council Educational Research and Training (NCERT) books and may translate/ print them with permission of the NCERT.

(f) They may indicate their requirement of NCERT books well in advance to forward the benefit of economy of scale to students and ensure that the books are provided in time.

(g) The state boards may approach the CBSE to share the question papers to bring uniformity in assessment and evaluation.

(h) The state boards decided to constitute Inter Board Working Group (IBWG) comprising Chairpersons, Board of Gujarat, Jammu & Kashmir, Kerala, Telangana, Chhattisgarh, Manipur, ICSE with Chairperson, CBSE as the Convener of the IBWG.

Consequent to these decisions, respective state governments dispensed with 'spiking' of marks in the name of moderation. In Karnataka, the pass percentage dropped by around 8%. The Union Minister even complimented the state government for biting the bullet. In Punjab, the pass percentage fell by more than 10%. Many other states chose to face the truth as well.

The CBSE was also one of the 'culprits' that had joined the bandwagon of 'spikers'. Consequent to the decision taken in the meeting held on 24 April, the organisation was then gearing up to do away with spiking. But, influential parents of the wards in Delhi were not prepared to give up the illusion of high percentage based on farcical spiking. Ironically the list included politicians, civil servants and advocates whose children had appeared in grade XII and were not prepared to give up the 'bonanza' of spike marks.

The media too got involved and the 'interested' parties managed to convey half-truths. A petition was filed in the High Court as well and it was alleged that the CBSE was changing the 'goal post' midway. It was difficult to fathom how doing away with across the board 'spiking' of marks could be construed as changing the goal post. The High Court ordered that moderation of marks should continue the way it had been done earlier. There was no mention of 'spiking' in the order. The CBSE chose to follow the orders in letter and spirit on the direction of the Union Minister. Everyone seemed to be happy as the pass percentage did not drop.

What was in fact sacrificed was a principled stand to do away with 'spiking'. To me, it was a huge embarrassment as we had failed to live up to our words.

Cheaters teaching the teachers

It was a known fact that everyone condemned the Bachelor in Education (B. Ed) and Diploma in Elementary Education (D.El.Ed)qualifications. Those existed only in names. The National Council for Teacher Education (NCTE) was powerful but there were allegations of corruption against it. Teachers' training institutions were mushrooming all over the country, thanks to the demand for teachers created by the Centrally Sponsored Scheme (CSS) of Sarva Shiksha Abhiyan (SSA) and the enactment of the RTE Act. By 2017, there were around 18,000 Teacher Education Institutions (TEI) in the country. Many of these institutions guaranteed a degree without attendance or internal assessments, of course for a fee. It was rumoured that some of them even guaranteed pass marks in the University examinations as well as employment as a part of a 'package deal'. This had assumed menacing proportions and it was eating into the essence of the education system in the country.

The pathetic state of affairs was officially recognised by the Justice Verma Commission (JVC) that was set up by the Supreme Court of India. It had the following report regarding the abysmal state of teacher education—

"The Teacher Eligibility Test (TET) instituted in 2011 as an essential criterion for teacher recruitment over and above a professional degree in teacher education has clearly demonstrated that the bulk of candidates who take the TET (conducted centrally as well as state-wise) do not qualify to be recruited, despite having a professional degree in teaching".

The TET pass percentage (13%) reflected the crisis of quality in the teacher education in the country. The Commission made several recommendations to reform teacher education and the Supreme Court made them mandatory. One of these was that the NCTE should establish its own Teacher Education and Accreditation Centre. At the time these recommendations were made, the NCTE had already been doing accreditation. In fact, it had been doing so since 2002, but it was through an outsourced arrangement with the National

Assessment and Accreditation Council (NAAC), an autonomous institution of the University Grants Commission (UGC). The NAAC's mandate was to provide assessment and accreditation services for institutions of higher learning under the regulatory control of the UGC. Since Teacher Education Institutions were not under the ambit of the UGC, the work that the NAAC was doing on behalf of the NCTE was not its core function. Since 2002 (when the MOU was signed between the NCTE and the NAAC) until 2017, it had accredited only 1522 TEIs. Besides implementing the Supreme Court mandate on the JVC, there arose the question of whether the framework for accreditation used by the NAAC was suitable for accrediting TEIs as well. Finally, the NAAC expressed its inability in 2013 to undertake the humongous task of accrediting TEIs. Yet it continued since the NCTE was not able to finalise a bespoke framework for accrediting TEIs or set up its own centre as mandated by the Supreme Court. Though several Supreme Court orders were sent out, the JVC remained unimplemented and this amounted to contempt of the Supreme Court; nothing happened because nobody went to court.

The arrival of Santhosh Mathew as Chairman NCTE in January 2017 changed the scenario. He made a sincere effort to fight corruption, benchmark teacher capability by reforming TET, build a national registry for all teachers and implemented several of the pending JVC mandates, most importantly capacity building of teacher educators (DIKSHA) and accreditation (TeachR). The steps he followed were:

1. The NCTE was made completely paperless through 100% adoption of e-office.
2. He obtained the approval of the Council for shifting all regional offices to the HQ in Delhi and mandating the development of an ERP software that would make it possible for all stakeholders to transact with the NCTE remotely through the internet.
3. India's first bespoke accreditation framework for TEIs–TeachR was developed. TeachR reduced the cost of accreditation for TEI's by 50% and made it possible for all 18000 TEIs to be accredited in one year. TeachR also introduced new elements in an accreditation framework such as:

(a) audio-video recording of an interview and one hour of teaching by teacher educators

(b) a standardised test for student teachers to test extent and quality of student learning in each TEI

4. Securing the services of the Quality Council of India (QCI) for collecting data and verifying claims by TEIs so that expert teacher educators carefully selected by the NCTE could peer review TEIs on a digital platform sitting in a central studio or remotely.
5. Establishing an IT platform which would continuously collect data from TEIs as digital exhaust on all important aspects of its functioning, including the use of a library, practice teaching videos by student teachers, lesson plans etc. making it possible for the NCTE to do a remote audit of regulatory compliance on a continuous basis.
6. Establishing DIKSHA—the national teacher portal that was launched by the Vice President of India on Teacher's Day 2017. DIKSHA is a capacity enhancement tool for teachers in schools, teacher educators and student teachers and a classroom teaching aid. It is designed for use even in the absence of internet connectivity. DIKSHA also has a built-in teacher registry that captures the full life cycle of a teacher from the moment s/he enters a TEI as a student teacher right through the days as a teacher and beyond.

Teachers will be able to use this to demonstrate excellence and move up the career ladder.

In 2016, the NCTE had launched an initiative that required TEIs to submit an affidavit indicating the extent to which they were compliant with the regulations, especially with respect to land, building and faculty. This was improved upon by introducing a computerised Mandatory Affidavit System (MAS) that required TEIs to complete all data fields before they submit. Those that did not submit the affidavit were to be issued a show cause notice. A notice was also issued to inform the public at large that students should seek admission only in such colleges as had submitted affidavits. The list of colleges that had submitted the affidavits was placed on the NCTE portal. Around 4000 colleges had not submitted the affidavit. This was a clear admission on their part that they only existed in names.

The new Chairperson had set the cat amongst the pigeons. The well-connected mafias of teachers' education got moving. More than 500 representations were moved against the new regime that sought to sift the 'dirty' wood and rate the rest of the colleges based on objective criterion. One of the contentions of the complainants related to the alleged accreditation by a third party, it was argued that the QCI was being tasked with the accreditation of colleges. This was contested on facts. The QCI was engaged to verify facts and not to grant accreditation that was to be done by the NCTE. The hiring of the QCI itself was challenged. The fee was questioned. The NCTE had satisfactory answers to all the questions but the Human Resource Development Minister, Mr Prakash Javadekar, usually very composed, was rattled. He was perhaps under pressure. There were a number of reviews held at the level of the Minister and his discomfort increased on each occasion.

Meanwhile, I was sounding the state governments about the move by the NCTE. The Chief Minister of UP, Mr Yogi Adityanath wholeheartedly welcomed the idea to clean up the mess. He conceded the fact that there would be pressure on him as well but promised all support. The Chief Minister of Rajasthan, Mrs Vasundhara Raje Scindia gave me a standing ovation as I spelt out the plan of action in a conference at Jaipur. The West Bengal Government, normally at war with the centre, supported the move wholeheartedly and came out with an advertisement. Almost every other state recognised the menace and supported the move.

The media, usually critical, backed the plan of action. In a news item, 'The Sordid Tale of Teacher Education in India,' the *Mint* wrote about 'How the NCTE presided over the development of what is perhaps the weakest teacher education system in any large country in the world'. The paper went on to add that the power of the NCTE was used to 'drive a system of graft where colleges licences were sold'. It expressed hope in the process that was being put in place—'The MHRD and NCTE are now doing something that most of us had only hoped for'.

The Bihar High Court directed the NCTE to carry out the inspection of colleges in the state. The initial inspections overlooked glaring shortcomings that were revealed later when the status in some of the colleges was filmed with the help of the QCI. These subsequent inspections revealed a pathetic state of affairs. But the TEI's moved the Bihar High Court saying that the Chairperson NCTE had committed contempt of court because among other things he had used the QCI. The court took an adverse view and even asked the MHRD to file an affidavit on how the Chairperson could be removed. Things deteriorated rapidly, and the court indicated that it was inclined to initiate criminal contempt against the Chairperson. The Chairperson was saved in the nick of time when the Supreme Court in a bench presided over by the Chief Justice ordered that the case be transferred to itself.

Over 230 cases were filed in different High Courts of the country by then, asking that the draft TeachR framework should stay. Although most High Courts refused to grant a stay, three did. This was detrimental because when on the order of the Supreme Court all cases were transferred to the Delhi High Court, the court took a view that it should put all cases in an even keel and therefore started granting stays to all those who approached it. This must have been one of the first cases in the Indian legal history in which even before the policy had been finalised, i.e. at the draft stage itself, the courts intervened and stayed proceedings. What makes this case even more interesting from a jurisprudence point of view is the fact that the stay that had been granted by the High Courts is against the implementation of the orders of the Supreme Court.

In the final analysis, while I am sure that the initiatives taken by the NCTE will get the go-ahead from both the courts and from the government, it is anybody's guess as to how long it will take for that to happen. In the meantime, the NCTE efforts to implement the mandate of the Supreme Court with regards to the JVC has been successfully blocked by TEIs through clever retail litigation.

The loss is India's.

The Right to Education Act:
Did it serve the purpose?

When the British left this country, they took justice with them and left behind laws, in-laws and outlaws. We have a mindset that makes us believe enacting legislation is a panacea for all ills. The RTE Act was born out of this mindset. I have often wondered why the executive needs a law to do something which it is authorised to do in any case under the extant legal provisions.

Let us try to understand the purpose of the RTE Act and then try to answer the following:

1. Whether the purpose could have been served without the law?
2. Whether the purpose was served because of enactment of the RTE Act?
3. Whether the RTE Act made it more difficult and complicated to deliver a quality education?

In the Statement of Objects and Reasons of the Act, the enactment seeks to ensure:

(a) that every child has the right to be provided full-time elementary education of satisfactory and equitable quality in a formal school which satisfies certain essential norms and standards;

(b) 'compulsory education' casts an obligation on the appropriate government to provide and ensure admission, attendance and completion of elementary education;

(c) 'free education' means that no child, other than a child who has been admitted by his or her parents to a school which is not supported by the appropriate government, shall be liable to pay any kind of fee or charges or expenses which may prevent him or her from pursuing and completing elementary education;

(d) the duties and responsibilities of the appropriate governments, local authorities, parents, schools and teachers in providing free and compulsory education; and

(e) a system for protection of the right of children and a decentralised grievance redressal mechanism.

In short, the goal is to provide free and compulsory quality education. By enacting a law, the government has imposed upon itself a legal and enforceable obligation. However, how does it help? The government could (should) have provided free quality education without any law as has been done in a number of countries in the world. No one was stopping the government from doing that. In fact, successive governments were trying to do that but were unable to do so. The inability was certainly not because of absence of legislation. In fact, enactment of legislation hardly led to any improvement in the delivery of quality education. As mentioned earlier, the learning outcomes came down during the years that followed the legislation.

The legislation made the task of delivering quality education complex and difficult. The focus of the Act is primarily on 'inputs' (like infrastructure) rather than 'outcomes'. It has created an adversarial role between 'public' and 'private' schools. The Act mandates under section 12(1)(c) that even private schools "shall admit in Class I, to the extent of at least twenty five per cent of the strength of that class, children belonging to weaker section and disadvantaged group". The way reimbursement is to be provided has created a number of problems. The norms and standards prescribed in the schedule for a school are far removed from ground reality. What is perhaps desirable has been made mandatory. This has resulted in a phenomenal increase in the number of teachers. During the year 2015-16, there were 39,608 government schools that had fewer than 10 children but each school was supposed to have a minimum of two teachers. The budget private schools, most of which are doing a fantastic job of imparting education, are under enormous pressure to meet the prescribed standards or face closure. No attempt was made while enacting this legislation to look at the ground reality. The consequences have been disastrous. The focus has primarily been on regulation (legislations are perhaps meant for that) and not on development. Consequently, even after eight years of enactment, the country is no better than what it was.

The RTE Act has done more damage to the delivery of education. Section 16 of the Act provides that "No child admitted in a school shall be held back in any class or expelled from school till completion of elementary education".

The 'expulsion' part can be understood but not holding back a child in a class has meant that a large number of children are getting promoted without acquiring necessary attributes. The model of 'no detention' was apparently picked up from the West and transplanted in this country without considering the objective conditions obtaining here. Yet again the consequences have been devastating as there is a huge bottleneck at Class X level where the pass percentage has plummeted. The states were not even given the freedom to take a call on the issue. The government has subsequently decided to give an option to the states and the amendment is under the consideration of the parliament.

The penal provisions under the Act are outlined under section 18(5):

"Any person who establishes or runs a school without obtaining certificate of recognition or continues to run a school after withdrawal of recognition, shall be liable to fine which may extend to one lakh rupees and in case of continuing contraventions, to a fine of ten thousand rupees for each day during which such contravention continues".

In so many years there is hardly any school that has been penalised under this clause. Schools are violating the norms with impunity making a mockery of the legislation. Whereas on the one hand, the budget private schools continue to suffer because of pressure and harassment, the mafias running private schools purely on commercial lines are getting away with blue murder. The Act cannot itself be blamed for this malaise, but it has done little to correct this malaise.

Education as a tool for resolving the J&K crisis

Pelting of stones at the police and paramilitary forces has added a new dimension to the Kashmir problem. Several government schools were also set on fire in the valley. These developments are extremely disturbing and have further complicated a complex scenario in the state. Could education be used as a tool to bring back the state from the brink? Was it possible to 'mainstream' children through such an instrument and to prevent them from 'straying'? It was a challenging task but well worth considering.

A 'Roadmap for Transforming School Education' for the state of Jammu & Kashmir was drafted in consultation with the experts and state officials. The roadmap first identified the problems relating to education in the state:

1. Comparatively low (and decreasing) enrollment in government and aided schools

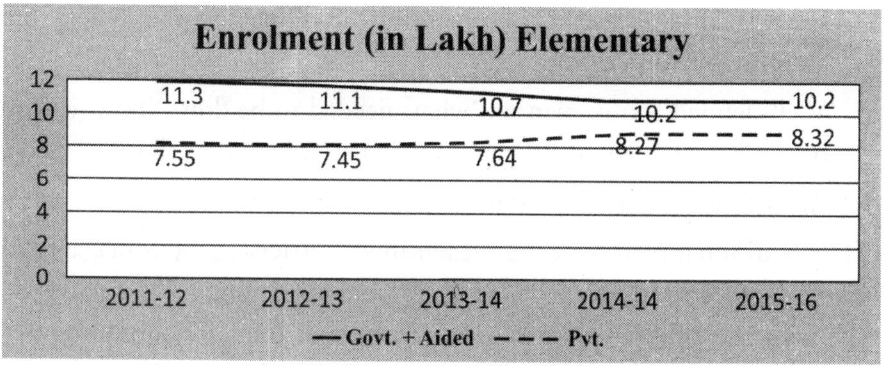

(Source: UDISE, NIEPA)

2. A considerable number of out of school children
3. High drop-out rates with an annual average dropout rate of 6.79% at the primary level well above the national average of 4.17%
4. Learning outcomes low and well below the national average and decreasing

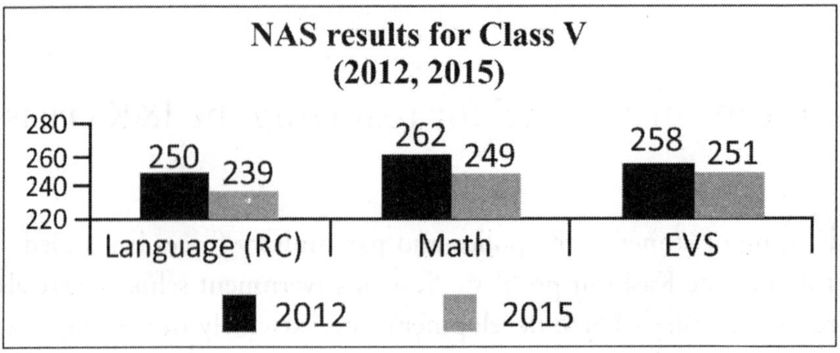

(Source: NCERT, NAS Surveys)

The Roadmap focused on the following aspects:

1. A strong governance structure of the reform initiative with project management support to review and implement key initiatives.
2. Context-specific initiatives and interventions which had worked in other parts of the country.
3. Holistic plan to improve key enablers, overhauling the human resource systems, driving quality interventions and making the system more accountable to performance.
4. Well-defined action plan on 'what' needed to be done, 'how' it would be done, 'who' would do it and by 'when' it would be done.
5. An additional plan for certain identified districts.

The additional plan for certain identified districts of the Srinagar Valley was considered critical in the context of 'mainstreaming'. The idea was to engage with the children from schools in these districts for sustaining peace and the plan entailed the following:

(i) revival of dysfunctional schools
(ii) one-to-one school linkage program
(iii) improvement of digital infrastructure in priority schools
(iv) smart card-based health insurance scheme for teachers
(v) introduction and use of solar energy in priority schools

(vi) promoting emotional well-being and career readiness

(vii) adoption of the NCERT syllabus and CBSE affiliation in schools

Personal visits to interior parts of the state, including the valley, helped me appreciate the ground reality. The proposed plan was discussed with the Governor who appreciated the approach, especially the part relating to linkage of schools in the valley with those in other parts of the country. The idea herein was to connect each school in 'priority' districts of the valley to a 'sister' school in another part in the country. Each paired school would be mentored by an NGO which would facilitate the partnership and exchange between the schools. It was believed that increased interaction with peer groups will lead to a richer exchange of ideas, an experience of cultural integration and natural respect for the differences in the two peer groups. The exchange would also provide a sense of association and support to the schools involved.

The school 'linkage' programme would also include improvement in digital infrastructure in such schools. These facilities would enable virtual exchange programmes before physical exchange and e-learning content for students.

I was pleasantly surprised when the Chief Minister readily agreed to adopt the NCERT syllabus and curriculum in the state government schools.

In my understanding, this would go a long way in enabling young and impressionistic minds in understanding the national context. There was also a willingness to affiliate schools with the CBSE. She seemed to appreciate the efficacy of and utility of CBSE examinations and it would equip the child with a greater chance for qualifying in the engineering and medical entrance tests.

A workshop was planned at Srinagar with NGOs to outline their role in the roadmap for J&K. There was an initial reluctance on the part of NGOs for obvious reasons and only a couple of them agreed to participate. However, soon they realised that the government meant business. Finally, as many as 31 participated. These discussions took place in Srinagar, not very far from where an encounter with terrorists was underway. However, this did not deter the enthusiasm of the participants who fully endorsed the proposed approach and their role thereunder. All the stakeholders, the central government, the state government and the NGOs were now on board and committed to taking the project forward. Steering Committees were constituted at the central and state level. The first meeting of the Central Steering Committee was held within a month and action could be seen on the ground. The state government had moved a proposal for the affiliation of four state government schools to the CBSE. Approval was granted to the 'School Linkage Programme'. It was also decided that except the funds required for setting up of new Kendriya Vidyalayas and Navodaya Vidyalayas and for the proposed health insurance scheme for teachers, the other proposals could be funded under the ongoing schemes.

A beginning had been made.

Digital revolution in Pashtepada

It was an incredible sight as I walked into this zila parishad school in a village called Pashtepada. This was during my first visit to Maharashtra as Secretary, School Education and Literacy, Government of India. An officer, not from Maharashtra, had suggested that I should visit Pashtepada. The proud teacher, Sandeep Gund had received me and took me around the school that was now totally digital even in the absence of regular electric supply.

Pashtepada is a small hamlet, situated 40 km from block headquarters at Shahapur and 80 km from the district headquarters Thane. Sandeep Gund got his first posting in this village, with a population of 350, as a zila parishad primary teacher. The village was hard to reach as the last bus halt was in a village 2 km away. Still, the teacher was eager to start his work. When he reached his destination, he saw a neglected school building and barely 50% attendance of the enrolled children. Neither children nor the parents expected much from the school and its teachers. But Gund was optimistic and had bright dreams for his students.

Noticing that the children were fascinated by the screen and moving images, Gund decided to use the computer as a learning tool. He said, "As a teacher, I decided to focus on what interests the children the most. Self-interest leads to willingness to learn, ensures physical and mental participation and concentration crucial in the learning process". He got an old computer as donation from an NGO, the first digital tool in this school. Experimenting on a computer he developed simple learning lessons, screened films, and made PPTs to show to the children. A TV set like device attracted children to the school.

Gund succeeded in achieving complete attendance with this first step. For better use of technology, he carried out his own research, found out what made it effective, and its merits and demerits. He developed his own method of Activity Based Digital Learning (ABDL), the innovation that got him state award and recognition.

Today the students in Pashtepada zila parishad school are free from schoolbags. Each child has a tablet with pdf textbooks and references uploaded on them. Individual tablets also store student's worksheets and the projects they undertake in the school. This has enabled evaluation. Examinations are conducted online. Hence the results are instant. The students do their homework in notebooks so that their writing skills are retained and improved.

Self-learning is encouraged. Screen-sharing by teacher and students, as well as sharing of e-content, is how the classroom transactions take place. Learning from their surrounding environment is also promoted. Students create videos based on their field projects.

Tablets are also used as recording devices to record lectures, classroom activities and answers by students in their own voices. Sometimes they can take the tablet home so that family can see the content and performance of their children on a tablet or by connecting it to their TV. It was felt necessary to share what goes on in the school with parents.

The school is now well-equipped with digital devices like interactive smart boards, IR Camera, interactive projector, interactive monitor, e-desk, e-podium, and has digital content library with wi-fi connectivity accessible to students. It has also put in place a content development studio. Global virtual classes and tours are conducted as well.

All these systems run on solar energy, with a one-time investment of INR 1.25 lakh. The solar unit is portable, as the panels are foldable. Once charged the school devices can run for 5-6 hours.

Based on his research of students' performances, Gund has noted the benefits of digital learning. It helps to accelerate comprehension, improves retention, and makes children's attendance regular and consistent. The parents and community are happy with these changes, as they feel assured that their children's future will be brighter with digital education.

Gund later prepared a blueprint for a digital smart school.

However, the upgradation took place gradually as it was dependent on availability of funds. The primary support for this came from the community through cash donation and labour. They were joined by a few NGOs and other donors.

A self-motivated pilot of digital school had the potential of being replicated and upscaled across the state through the support and encouragement of the School Education Department.

Maharashtra State Government launched the Pragat Shaikshanik Maharashtra (PSM) initiative to improve the achievements of school children. The PSM was conceived in response to the appeal by the then Chief Minister of the state, Devendra Phadanvis, who focused on quality education as one major goal in Key Responsibility Areas (KRAs) he had set for the state. Accordingly, the State Education Minister Vinod Tawade initiated the formation of a comprehensive programme PSM with Nand Kumar, Principal Secretary, School Education.

The PSM showcased best practices of learning across the state. Gund became one of the active members of the 'Techno-savvy Teachers—a group of self-motivated digital teachers in schools who led the digital school movement in Maharashtra.

For me, there were many learnings from the visit to the zila parishad school. Gund had clearly shown that it could be done. It was a story that could be told. It was an effort that was replicable, scalable and sustainable. It had the potential to transform the delivery of education even in remote areas of the country through use of technology.

The Digital School Movement in Maharashtra has picked up. Over 89% of government schools are equipped with digital learning and over INR 326 crores have been raised through crowd sourcing to upgrade the schools. This success is owed to the persistent efforts of teachers like Sandeep Gund, who paved the way for digital education in government schools when it was beyond imagination for many.

Any news is bad news ... or they will make it appear like one

'NCERT textbook has a chapter on Naxalite leader Kishenji', screamed a leading English daily. The news item was published on 30 May 2017. The reference was to one Kishenji, a Naxal leader, who was killed by COBRA battalion in an encounter near Bengal–Jharkhand border on 24 November 2011. It further stated that 'NCERT is now coming under fire for allegedly dedicating a page to Naxalite leader Kishenji'.

Given the fact that the news was published in a leading English daily, it was taken as gospel truth. There was pandemonium and explanations were called for. What was published was believed to be true.

This item was related to the content on page 76, chapter 6 of the NCERT Class X Political Science textbook, *Democratic Politics-II.* The chapter discusses the role of political parties in the rise of democracy, formation of constitutional designs and working of governments. On page 76, the matter under the heading 'A moral force in politics?' contains content in the form of an imaginary conversation. Here, four women leading very powerful people's movements in different parts of the country discuss ideas of Kishenji regarding the role of political organisations. According to him, a fundamental social transformation, or basic change in any aspect of life of the people, is possible only through political organisations.

This textbook was published in March 2007. The inspiration behind this narrative on page 76 was Shri Kishen Patnaik (1930-2004), who was elected as a Member of Parliament from Sambalpur, Odisha in 1962. He occupied the role of an elder statesman. The integrity of his personal life and absence of falsehoods in his intellectual commitment helped the younger generations to see in him the elderly activist they no longer found in mainstream politics. He passed away in 2004.

The correspondent didn't care to crosscheck the facts and went ahead with the story generating a lot of paperwork and misunderstanding.

When facts were brought to the notice of the newspaper there was no apology forthcoming. It was merely published as the NCERT's 'version' of the story. Only media can take the liberty of publishing different 'versions' of truth and get away with it.

What's gone wrong with the education sector? Is there a way out?

Except getting most of the children to school, everything that could go wrong has gone wrong with school education in India. The situation is alarming, and the time bomb is ticking. Unfortunately, this is not perceived as a crisis because there is no perceptible epidemic. Hence, the decision makers are allowing these wounds to fester. Like in many schemes of the government, there is a lot of 'chintan' (thinking) but hardly any action. For any action, there has first to be acceptance of a crisis at hand. There must be a realisation of the mistakes that are being currently made. There must be a defined action plan that is politically acceptable, socially desirable, technologically feasible and financially viable. There is no need for a policy. There are too many of them. What is needed is an action plan. What needs to be done? How will it be done? Who will do it and by when will it be done? In a democracy, the ultimate decision maker is the political executive. (It is a different matter that courts are gradually nibbling away this turf as well.) Unfortunately, in India, the education sector has gotten politicised and the teacher is treated as a political tool. Political decision making is centred around use of these tools for political ends rather in improving the state of affairs. Without the political will to set things right, nothing will work. The NDA government had that mandate. Whether this mandate was getting translated into action is a million-dollar question. In the initial years, the attention given to education has left a lot to be desired. The budgetary allocations actually came down and there were as many as five different officers that headed the Department of School Education in the first two and half years of the government.

On the financial allocation front, there were many other problems.

Section 7 of the RTE has the following provision: Sharing of financial and other responsibilities:

1. The central government and the state governments shall have concurrent responsibility for giving funds for carrying out the provisions of this Act.

2. The central government shall prepare the estimates of capital and recurring expenditure for the implementation of the provisions of the Act.
3. The central government shall provide to the state governments, as grants-in-aid of revenues, such percentage of expenditure referred to in sub-section (2) as it may decide, from time to time, in consultation with the state governments.
4. The central government may make a request to the President to make a reference to the Finance Commission under sub-clause (d) of clause (3) of article 280 to examine the need for more resources to be provided to any state government so that the said state government may provide its share of funds for carrying out the provisions of the Act.
5. Notwithstanding anything contained in sub-section (4), the state government shall, taking into consideration the sums provided by the central government to a state government under sub-section (3), and its other resources, be responsible to provide funds for implementation of the provisions of the Act.
6. The central government shall—(a) develop a framework of national curriculum with the help of academic authority specified under section 29; (b) develop and enforce standards for training of teachers; (c) provide technical support and resources to the state government for promoting innovations, researches, planning and capacity building.

Thus, under the law, the central government can allocate 'such percentage of expenditure ... as it may determine'.

The schemes, including the SSA are structured in a manner that 60% of the allocation should come from the centre and remaining 40% from the states (for states in the North Eastern Region and Jammu & Kashmir, it is 90% for the centre and 10% for the states).

However, the ground reality is that the central government supports only 30 to 40% of the outlay. The states have been crying hoarse (evidenced by the number of letters written in this regard) but to no avail. This situation was partly under control as there was a stipulation for earmarking of funds for education in the allocations made by the 13th Finance Commission. However, though the allocations were substantially increased by the 14th Finance Commission, the earmarking for education was dispensed with. This has created a serious crisis.

The central government has a choice to formally reduce its contribution and align it to actual contribution, but it is perhaps politically unpalatable. Hence, we continue with the charade of contributing 60% while the actual contribution is around half of this.

The problem is not merely with finances which indeed is a huge issue. The real problem of education in the country centres around government teachers. It begins with the pre-service training of teachers (outlined in 'Cheaters Teaching the Teachers'). The selection of teachers itself is a tricky affair. No wonder an ex-Chief Minister finds himself in jail. States and politicians have found ways to shell out patronage. In 2017, there were more than 11 lakh teachers who were teaching but did not have requisite qualifications to teach. These teachers should have been thrown out as per the stipulations of the RTE Act, but the Act was amended to provide another window to such teachers to acquire necessary qualifications. In fact, the period of Diploma of Elementary Education (D.El.Ed) was squeezed from 24 months to 18 months to accommodate these teachers.

A study has revealed that 25% to 30% to these highly paid school teachers do not go to the schools. The problem is more acute in the northern states where politics has gotten the better of education. Teachers have found unique ways to ensure that they are not hauled up for being absent. There are 'substitute' teachers who are paid by the regular teacher to be present on their behalf. Then there are standard/undated leave applications with the controlling officers who collude in this whole drama. There are exceptions in the form of exceptional teachers but the sense of security among the government teachers and the consequent lack of sense of responsibility amongst majority of them has had a devastating impact.

Transfers of teachers is a major 'industry' and a primary pre-occupation of politicians. A lot of the time of the civil servants is also spent on managing these transfers and in attending to service matters, most of which end up in courts. Education is gradually getting reduced to a sector of the teachers, for the teachers and by the teachers.

The key question is how to get around these problems. There can be a solution, but one has to think out of the box.

The annual expenditure per child in government schools is around INR 18,000. Can this amount be better utilised for improved learning outcomes in the child?

Several studies have revealed that even the poor parents are prepared to pay for schooling. Many of them are already doing it. James Tooley in his well-researched book *The Beautiful Tree* clearly states that since the quality of education in parent-funded private schools exceeds that provided by the government sector, the corollary social benefits of education would be commensurately greater as well. He concludes, after an in-depth analysis, that the "private schools ... appear to be superior to government schools in the creation of public goods". The author researched and found that "there were schools in almost every village before the British replaced them with the system that provided the foundations of today's public systems". Tooley blames the British Government for uprooting *The Beautiful Tree* and he mentions Mahatma Gandhi's address at the Royal Institute of International Affairs in London in 1931 to buttress his argument. The British uprooted the private education system that served the poor as well as the rich and left India 'more illiterate than it was fifty or a hundred years ago' as ... 'they crowded out the already flourishing private education system'.

Tooley quotes from PROBE (Public Report on Basic Education in India, 1999) while explaining the secret of success in private schools: "In a private school, the teachers are accountable to managers (who can fire them), and, through him or her, to the parents (who can withdraw their children). In a government school, the chain of accountability is much weaker, as teachers have a permanent job with salaries and promotions unrelated to performance". This observation is also borne out by the National Achievement Survey conducted by NCERT in the year 2015. The survey concluded that 'the privately managed schools performed better than the government and government aided schools'.

The public and private schools co-exist in the country but there is an adversarial relationship between the government functionaries and the private schools. Instead of hounding the private schools or threatening to hound them, should we not think in terms of evolving a model where healthy competition between the two sectors can be used for imparting quality education giving value to every penny that the government spends on school education? The school voucher system has been tried in a few countries and with some success. Why not provide entitlement to a child in the form of a voucher or a debit card that he/she can utilise in an empanelled public or private school? Quality of school can be ensured through the process of empanelment. This can be done and, perhaps, should be done. However, it would need some political will to do it. It is high time we began doing so.

Standing by Colleagues : A Price Worth Paying

Supporting a just cause

It was 2003. I had just returned from central deputation. The state of Uttar Pradesh had gone down many notches in terms of administration. I was posted there as Secretary, Department of Horticulture. The Minister of the department had a dubious reputation. Right at the beginning of my tenure in this new assignment, I received a '*firman*' (order) from him. The instruction was clear and in writing— an officer of the Directorate of Horticulture in the state was to be suspended. But, no reason was assigned for it. I knew the officer and had admired him for his efficiency and integrity (a rare set of qualities in a state that was known for corruption). I asked the Minister about the reason for such a precipitate action. What he stated was surprising to me. The Minister was hell-bent on suspending the officer because the officer had not paid him a visit. The reason was not adequate. However, I spoke to the concerned officer to ascertain his version of the story. He stated that he had met the Minister on a number of occasions but not the way he wanted. The Minister was expecting *nazrana* from the officer. This development was brought to the notice of the Chief Secretary as I was not willing to propose suspension of an officer who had not met the Minister the way he desired. The Chief Secretary was kind enough to suggest a way out. As per the extant practice, in case of strong disagreement with the Minister, I could route the file through the Chief Secretary, which I did. A strong case was made against suspending the officer and the file was sent to the Chief Secretary who never sent it to the Minister (Red tape could help sometimes!) The Minister continued to fret and fume but couldn't gather the courage to broach the issue with the Chief Secretary who was known to be a forthright officer.

The officer was never suspended much to the frustration of the Minister who ultimately got me transferred on some other pretext. By this time, one had come to accept the fact that for a civil servant, transfer, like death, was inevitable.

Another reward

Pradeshiya Investment Corporation of Uttar Pradesh (PICUP) was turned around in 2005. The Phoenix had risen from the ashes. However, the revival of this financial institution meant that it could now be 'milked' again. Other demands were also made on the institution. The Chief Minister faced enormous pressure to shift me out as I was unwilling to toe the line of an 'immortal lion' who ran the show. It surprised everyone that I was not shifted immediately. It took a scheming civil servant to get me shifted to the post of Commissioner, Rural Development.

Once the Chief Minister was conducting regional reviews with regards to rural development. One such meeting was held at Allahabad and he praised the effort being made in this region. However, later in the afternoon, he apparently announced the suspension of a few junior officers. I got to know of it through the newspaper the next morning. I did not take any action as no formal order was communicated. The Secretary to the Chief Minister called me and asked me the reason for not suspending the officers of my department who were on the list announced by the CM in his press conference. The tone was threatening. Everything seemed to have gone smoothly at the meeting and there was no inkling of any suspension. However, there had to be some news to hit the headlines and everything smooth would have made no news.

As was the fashion those days there had to be few sacrificial lambs (read officers) for slaughter. A lengthy list of officers on the suspension roll would have served the dual purpose of making news as well as warning the officers to toe the line. This is what was done. Their crime was not known. In fact, the Secretaries and the Head of the Departments were asked to dig out charges against those that were being suspended. They were, therefore, being condemned without trial. 'Justice' (if you can use that phrase) was delivered in a way that put the medieval world to shame.

Some bureaucrats chose to toe the line, perhaps fearing reprisals or expecting rewards. I was in no mood to relent and gave it back to the 'powerful' Secretary.

He initially returned fire with threats of dire consequences. However, soon realising that threats had no effect on me, he profusely apologised for such utterances. I not only refused to suspend officers without due examination but also refused to dig out charges against those that were proposed to be suspended at higher levels in the government. It was certainly a risk but risk well worth taking.

Next morning, I volunteered to shift out of the post of Commissioner, Rural Development. The government too was willing to accede to my request as my presence in the Department would have proved embarrassing to them.

On the suspension front, the government was going great guns. Condemning and shooting down helpless bureaucrats with the help of those that were powerful and willing became an engaging pastime. Hence, mass suspension continued to hit the news. However, the saving grace was that the officers of the Rural Development Department were not a part of the list when the next review took place at Gorakhpur. I did not know whether my letter to the Principal Secretary to the Chief Minister contributed to the mitigation in the misery heaped upon the officers in the mad rush for mass suspension, but I took comfort from the fact that I had responded to the voice of my conscience and that was rewarding enough for me.

Choosing to stand by Mr Harish Chandra Gupta

Right through my career, I tried to stand by my colleagues, especially those who were put to harassment for no fault of theirs. Two such instances stand out.

Questions were asked of me when, as Coal Secretary, Government of India, I chose to defend Mr H C Gupta, an IAS officer of 1971 batch and ex-Coal Secretary, who had been charge-sheeted along with others in several cases relating to coal block auctions. A variety of questions emanated from those who hardly had any knowledge of the facts and from my well-wishers who questioned my desire to stick my neck out.

Well, first of all, I firmly believed that Mr Harish Chandra Gupta was not wrong. No Secretary could/should be held responsible for not verifying facts that were not apparently erroneous on the face of the record. If this is mandated in administration, all decision making would come to a grinding halt.

Secondly, I was convinced that there was no mala fide or criminal intent in any of the allegations levelled against him. This was also borne out in the judgements against Mr Gupta. In one of the judgements, it was clear that neither it was alleged by the prosecution nor any evidence was made available to show that Mr Gupta obtained allocation of a coal block for the accused company by any corrupt or illegal means.

Finally, I did it because Mr H C Gupta had enjoyed a spotless reputation as an officer, and I was a witness to it. Moreover, my personal belief is that if we hound the honest, the society and the administration will be left with either dishonest performers or deceitful non-performers.

The decision to stand by and support Mr Gupta was a personal one, born out of convictions and, hence, I was not bothered about the price to be paid in this regard. I was not sure whether I paid a price for being forthright and upfront in going the distance but felt contented that I did my bidding as per my conscience.

The CBSE exam paper leak

The defence of Mrs Anita Karwal, Chairperson, Central Board of Secondary Education (CBSE) was a different context altogether. The CBSE is an institution of the central government under the Ministry of Human Resource Development (MHRD) to conduct examinations for classes 10 and 12 for such schools that are affiliated to the board. It has evolved as an institution of repute with more than 20,000 schools affiliated to the board and many more in the queue seeking affiliation. Anita Karwal, who had taken over as its Chairperson a few months before the 'Paper Leak Crisis', had started her work by taking on some of those with vested interests that had pushed the Board into a business that was lucrative for those groups. One such 'business' was the publication of books that was primarily the domain of National Council for Educational Research and Training. Karwal promptly stopped this practice that did 'hurt' a few people.

The 2018 board examination commenced on 5 March. On 15 March, the Chairperson and few other officials of the board received a WhatsApp message from someone in the media, indicating a leaked Accountancy Question Paper (QP). With rumours spreading thick and fast through social media, it created panic. The Controller of Examination in the CBSE who was tasked with conducting the examinations immediately got it verified from the Regional Offices. The idea was to ascertain whether the packets containing the QPs were sealed before they were opened. On being informed that the packets were not tampered with, it was decided a complaint should be registered with Delhi Police. The matter was examined at length. Reports relating to leak were discarded on two counts. The QPs were found sealed before the commencement of examinations, and it could be safely assumed that the students (examinees) were inside their classrooms by the time this purported leak took place. The students, therefore, had no access to information about the QPs at such an advanced hour. Even if a handful of them did have access, the probability of their being able to utilise this information for undue gains, was very little.

Posting an image of the QP on social media just before the actual distribution of the same to the examinees appeared more to be an attempt to create panic. A QP of Accountancy was floating around in the Dehradun Regional Office area as well. However, on verification, it was found to be fake. Similarly, a couple of leaked papers of Accountancy were found on YouTube, which too on verification were found to be a hoax.

It was either done with an intent to destabilise the whole system or simply a crime related to corrupt practices with some ulterior motive. The possible motive to sully the reputation of CBSE through confusion and panic couldn't be ruled out.

On reviewing the episode, the Controller of Examination was directed by the Chairperson to go through the entire process carefully. The process also entailed a scrutiny of the role of the banks where the examination papers were housed in intense security. Several instructions were issued to strengthen the security and delivery system of question papers.

The design behind all this was quite evident then. Many unscrupulous elements seemed to have jumped into the bandwagon to take advantage of the situation and add fuel to fire. The electronic channels, in particular, started airing the news much after the examinations. The standard report talked about the availability of questions papers just before examinations. It appeared as if the electronic media was relishing the process of sensationalising the examinations. In all the cases nothing was found to substantiate these rumours. However, the panic continued.

YouTube videos devoted to solving purportedly leaked question papers of various subjects of classes 10 and 12 sprouted all over. All these channels were found to be hosting either very old or fake papers. An atmosphere of mistrust was deliberately created in the social media and rumour-mongers began to thrive.

In the backdrop of strict enforcement of exam by-laws, on 26 March 2018, a new modus operandi was found. The Economics QP of class 12 was rumoured to have leaked on the day of the exam. The rumours started taking ground after 10 am that day. The partial QP received on the WhatsApp of one of the officials was verified at around 10.30 am and it appeared to match with the actual QP for that day. It was gradually becoming evident that a handwritten paper that was similar or same as the actual QP was available much before the actual examination. An immediate enquiry was initiated to assess the spread and impact of this leak.

Later in the evening of 26 March, screenshots of few cell phones that had been purportedly used for circulating the said paper were received in an unmarked envelope. This was handed over to the police. A preliminary enquiry revealed that the paper had indeed been accessed by an unidentified section of students prior to the examinations. As the mode of circulation was social media, it could safely be assumed that this leak would have a very widespread reach.

While the issues relating to the Economics paper were being examined, another complaint regarding the leak of Class X Mathematics paper was received via email to the official email address of CBSE at 1.39 am on 28 March 2018. The mail was read at around 6.30 am. The Controller of Examination was immediately informed and was asked to investigate. When the Chairperson reached office at 8 am, the enquiry was still going on. Meanwhile, the Delhi Police was informed at 7 am. They were also requested to assess the spread of the leak. The said exam was to be taken by about 16 lakh students on 28 March. It was subsequently alleged that the Chairperson should have got it examined immediately. This was practically impossible because there is a Standard Operating Procedure (SOP) to open the strong room of the Controller of Examination to check question papers. No conclusion could have been arrived at without verifying whether there was a similarity between the purportedly leaked paper and the actual one and it would have been much worse to base any major decision on just a mail. As outlined earlier, a number of such papers that were purported to have been leaked in the past were actually a hoax. On detailed examination, it was found that a part of the email was the same as the actual question paper. This clearly implied that the miscreants behind this had access to the question papers a day before the examination.

The inference could be drawn at 10.30 am and the examinations had already commenced by then. It was difficult to stop the examination or verify whether students actually had access to the leaked paper. Regional Officers looking after Delhi and Haryana could confirm that there was a possibility of a leak in these states, but the rest of the ROs were unable to confirm the same. However, there was a good reason to believe that the papers had indeed been leaked and perhaps the leakage was widespread. The Human Resource Development Minister (HRM) was also informed by the Chairperson, CBSE about the developments. His response was quick and cryptic, "Order enquiry of leaks and attempts. Write to CBI also".

At about 3.30 pm that day the CBSE announced its decision to conduct the tests again for both the papers.

This was when the electronic media went ballistic. The media pressed the panic button for students, parents and schools. Attempts to bring any normalcy to the situation were severely hampered by continuous kite flying in both the print and electronic media. When HRM was briefed in the afternoon by the CBSE officials, he clearly instructed them not to speak a word to the media unless he permitted. He took the responsibility of handling the media but didn't address the media on this issue and made a passing reference to it in a media interaction organised for some other purpose. A cardinal mistake had been made.

By the evening of 28 March 2018, the media attack went vicious, malicious and personal. A lot of canards about the Chairperson in particular and the CBSE, in general, were deliberately spread by electronic media. A section of the media concluded and announced that the Chairperson had proceeded on leave during examinations. A news channel even sent their crew to Chairperson's erstwhile residence in Ahmedabad to check if she was hiding inside. She was hounded and trolled on social media and was called the PM's person, just because she belonged to the Gujarat cadre. It was a clear example of how low some sections of the media could stoop.

The Chairperson regularly informed me about the developments and the attempts made to manage the crisis. I suggested that she should clarify the situation to the media. But the instructions from the HRM were clear and the officials of the CBSE stayed away from the media. Unfortunately, I was away in Dehradun on 28 March to attend to my ailing father. He had to be brought to Delhi as he was in critical condition. On our way to Delhi in an ambulance with my father on 29 March, I tried to reach the Minister, Prakash Javadekar on phone but couldn't succeed. Hence, I had sent him a text message, "I feel that the Chairman should interact with media and keep them updated about the developments". He called back but there was no clarity about briefing the press. He was still non-committal. I messaged him again, "Thought over the whole issue. There is an impression going around that the Chairman of CBSE is hiding somewhere. I would suggest that she should speak to the media". Perhaps on account of being pushed, he did permit her to give a byte to the news channels. It was too complex an issue to be clarified through a byte and when that byte was given, it made confusion worse.

I reached Delhi. After admitting my father in a hospital, I focussed on the other crisis at hand and took the bull by the horns. I got an update from the Chairperson and then approached the Minister. He appeared jittery. The media was now hounding him as well and he was avoiding them. He suggested removal of Anita Karwal to contain the fallout. I had looked at the preliminary enquiry report. It clearly revealed that there was absolutely no fault on her part. In fact, she was in the midst of fighting a grim battle with the education mafia and a rampaging media. She had taken all possible steps to handle the situation. I decided to stand by her in this hour of crisis and take on the media myself. Unlike the Coal Ministry where Piyush Goyal had encouraged me to speak to the media, Javadekar was not as forthcoming. All media management in the ministry was done by the Minister himself. However, on this occasion, he seemed to be coming around to allow me to handle the media. But he wanted to take the PMO into confidence (A culture that had evolved over a period of time). A meeting was held at the PMO on 30 March. The PMO backed my stand and asked me to go ahead to brief the media later in the afternoon but only after I had received the PM's clearance through the PMO. I also suggested an announcement of the future course of action with regard to the two papers that had leaked. This too was agreed upon. We now had something concrete to tell the media. The Economics examination of class 12 was to be re-conducted and the decision on Mathematics paper for class 10 was to be taken subsequently on the basis of an enquiry into the extent and impact of leakage. The logic was simple. The class 10 examination was like an internal exam with virtually no implication on future admissions. Class 12 had much greater implications. (Subsequently, post enquiry, it was discovered that the class 10 paper leak was neither widespread nor did it have any impact on the outcome. Hence, no re-examination was conducted in this case and around 16 lakh children were saved from the trouble to appear again).

The press conference was originally scheduled at 5 pm on 30 March. The entire media was waiting for me but I was eagerly awaiting the clearance from the PMO. With every passing second, the suspense grew as everyone waited with bated breath. The clearance finally came at around 6 pm. This press conference was unarguably the toughest I ever had. Later I noted in my diary, "The Conference took place in the evening in a packed hall. The aggressive posture of the media reflected angst. Fortunately, in the hour-long interaction, I kept my cool and handled the questions reasonably well. One could clarify the approach of the government and the purpose seemed to have been served". It was perhaps much more than that. It was the severest of all tests in my career. I had not been able to protect Santosh Mathews but I could stand by another admirable (one of the finest I had come across in my career) officer, Anita Karwal.

Flight to Islamabad : So Near Yet So Far

I wanted to go but I was not particularly excited at the prospect. I was not even sure whether the visit to Islamabad in early 2007 for the World Bank Conference would come through. There were many clearances required: ranging from the political to the cadre. Then the Pak Mission in Delhi wanted all sorts of information. The road (read flight) to Pakistan was indeed a difficult one. That I did finally make it to the flight was nothing but a miracle. The fact, however, was that I was not really travelling to Pakistan on this flight. I was over-flying Pakistan. My intermediate destination was Dubai. To people elsewhere in the world who understood the geography of this region but not the politics of the subcontinent, it would sound strange, perhaps even ridiculous. But, that is how we have evolved over the past 60 years, on occasions even going to the extent of banning the overflights. The walls all over the world are coming down but we seem to be building new ones every day. It was quite inexplicable as were many other things when it came to the relationship between these two countries. I flew into Pakistan, finally, after having travelled a distance of fewer than a thousand kilometres in more than fifteen hours. Someone remarked, "You could have walked the distance in this time". But then good geography does not necessarily make for good politics. The Europeans took centuries and numerous bloody wars before realising that good geography and good politics could coexist. Good geography can indeed facilitate good politics. I do not really know how many centuries and how many more lives we would require to learn those lessons.

There was chaos at the Islamabad airport, reminiscent of the airports back in India, though marginally worse. The baggage took ages to come through. The immigration official gave me a suspicious look (fortunately that was the only suspicious look I had to suffer during the stay at Islamabad), and took her own time before stamping my passport. It was all very smooth thereafter. Despite the chaos, almost everyone was willing to help. Once they knew that I was from India, they were even more forthcoming. In their own unassuming way, they were busy demolishing the psychological barriers. I was almost immediately made comfortable. One of them accompanied me to a PCO to help me make a call to India. Folks at home had to be assured that I was safe and sound in an 'alien' country. The telecom revolution was yet to happen there. I paid through my nose for this call to India.

The drive to the Marriott Hotel took longer than expected. Traffic was quite disciplined and roads were wide. No one jumped the red light even during night (who says we cannot learn anything from Pakistan!). It is a different matter that most of the other regulations were flouted. The sight of a cop smoking right in front of the no-smoking sign was a great photo opportunity but I did not have a camera. Similarly, shops were open till late in the night despite a clear order to the contrary to save power.

Once inside the hotel, it is like anywhere in the world. The hotels, especially the five-star ones, have their own culture but the security around the hotel was disconcerting.

I had a sound sleep. The breakfast was sumptuous.

However, locating the ILO office was a different story. But, my cabbie was not flustered. He was polite and courteous. He was concerned about my persistent cough and even suggested some medicine. The drive with him was quite a revelation. He was convinced that the only way forward for the two countries was to make friends and to divert the expenditure from arms to development. He was talking sense, something that was ironically uncommon with those that could actively make a difference.

I thought I was late for the conference, having spent a lot of time locating the venue. However, I was wrong. The reception counter was still being readied when I arrived. The Indian subcontinent seems to have its own standard time. But, I was overwhelmed by the warmth shown by whoever I met. The inaugural session was marked by usual speeches but much shorter than the ones in India on such occasions (another lesson for the big brother). I made my presentation on the attempts being made in India to address issues relating to the workers in the unorganised sector. It seemed to have gone down well with the audience as, thereafter, I was treated like a hero with almost everyone wanting to know more about what was happening in this sector in India. There was also discussion about building synergies and learning from India.

A high ranking officer of the Pakistan Government took note of the inconvenience I was put to in the morning and I was immediately assigned a car. There were more revelations in store for me later in the afternoon. Another officer of the government took me around Islamabad. The sight of this lovely city from the mountaintop was gorgeous. He, however, confessed that this city did not reflect what Pakistan was. In fact, there is a saying that Islamabad is around 40 kilometres away from Pakistan. But, I was impressed. What he and the other residents of Islamabad had to say about the internal politics in Pakistan was even more interesting. They were concerned about the rampant corruption in top echelons. They wanted democracy in the country, but all political leaders had let them down. A sense of despondency was all pervasive. Almost all of them looked towards India with a lot of admiration, for its democratic traditions, for the sacrifice that some individuals had made in the recent past, for the development and growth in the recent past, for the IT revolution, for its education system and for the emerging opportunities. India was indeed shining in its neighbourhood even without an 'India shining' campaign. There was no rancour or jealousy. It was pure admiration and a yearning to emulate.

Contrary to the misconception we have in India about Pakistan, the media, both print and visual, was free and vibrant. The channels freely carried all the views and counterviews about the raging controversies involving the President and the Chief Justice of Pakistan. Almost all the newspapers were as caustic and critical about what was not right with the establishment. At least the fourth pillar of democracy was alive and kicking. Pakistan was evolving as a democracy in an unusual way. With its subcontinental flavour, it was different from other Islamic countries. Pakistan could perhaps provide democratic enlightenment to other Islamic countries in the region. (Can India help her do that?)

The women were not behind *burqas* as most of us believe in India. They were articulate and vocal. Most of the anchors on the TV channels were women who conducted themselves with professional ease. This might not be a representative sample, but it proved that there was no restriction on their mobility. The women there appeared to be as mobile as their counterparts in India. There was indeed no case for pontification at least on this front. The people on the streets looked at the Talibanisation of the Pakistani society with trepidation.

Articles after articles in the magazines betrayed such apprehensions and raised alarm against those who were attempting to push the country into the dark ages. The liberal majority needed to be understood and supported and not treated as a part of the fundamentalist minority.

It would be wrong to generalise what I saw and felt during the two-day and three-night long stay in Islamabad, but it was certainly better than forming an opinion on hearsay, as most of us do. It was heartening to see Lucknowee Tehzib in Islamabad. Being a Lucknowite, I could not help but be impressed. Everyone met you with a *Salaam Walekum* with smiles on their faces. I did not hear anyone shouting or losing his cool. Most of them were polite, and always willing to lend a helping hand. However, a laid-back attitude amongst the mass and skewed priorities at the top is taking a heavy toll on this beautiful and endearing country. As I departed from Islamabad, I was distressed by the fact that the airport of the capital city was so ill kept and so poorly managed.

Indian airports were also a matter of shame but India seems to be making an effort. Pakistan is perhaps still to wake up. They are still awaiting a Manmohan Singh (the Manmohan Singh of 1991 and not the Prime Minister) to redeem them. *Insha Allah*, this redemption will come about sooner than later for the wonderful people of this country. Perhaps the need of the hour is to learn from history and not to be obsessed with it, to learn from what is happening in and around the world, to get over the baggage of the past as quickly as possible and to look ahead because that is where the future lies, quite literally.

If I Were to Be Born Again

Having completed my innings in the Indian Administrative Service, I love to look back upon the years gone by with utmost satisfaction. There were several ups and downs (perhaps more ups than downs)— handling of the Babri Masjid agitation, the excitement and satisfaction of rolling out the RSBY, sorting out the 'coal' mess and grappling with education mafias are a few of those. And, that made life interesting. However, if I were to be born again and if I could make it (with the increasing competition and fewer vacancies), I would like to be an IAS officer yet again. The reason is simple. No other job on the earth gives you this much freedom and these many opportunities. This is one of the rare jobs where you can afford to remain honest in an increasingly vitiated socio-political environment. The Indian Administrative Service provides tremendous avenues for working towards public welfare and deriving immense satisfaction that more than compensates the comparative disadvantage in financial terms vis-à-vis a lucrative private sector assignment. Despite certain developments in the recent past, there is still a lot of authority vested in most of the positions occupied by an IAS officer during the course of his career. It is a different matter that some officers choose to abdicate this authority in lieu of some gain elsewhere. Whether they actually gain (at the cost of the service) or finally lose out is a moot point.

Ironically, the Indian Administrative Service has also the potential of shielding the corrupt. A few years ago, it was believed that the high and mighty could not be brought to book. However, thankfully, on account of informed public opinion and media glare, things are changing and at least some such bureaucrats are on the run.

The inefficient too can survive and even thrive. Once you pass the exam and keep your boss happy (not necessarily with good work), your promotions are secured. Though you may not reach the top (perhaps you may), you can still enjoy life, play badminton (now, golf) or indulge in some other activity till 09.00 hours, arrive at office at 10.30 hours, take lunch break for a couple of hours and return after a 'well-earned' siesta and then sit till late in the office to impress others how hard you work. In many states, if you are smart enough, then you can retain the official/earmarked residence for years in a city even after you occupy another house in another city consequent to your transfer. If you are smarter, you can have separate vehicles for the family at government cost. There would be many more such illustrations. Fortunately, very few bureaucrats fall in this category but the fact that some of us do enjoy such privileges indicates the availability of such options. No other service offers such 'facilities'.

All said and done, the IAS provides you an option to seek your own road to salvation. In fact, you not only can choose your own road, you can redefine 'salvation'. You can perform and exist; you may do nothing but still exist. You may survive if you are honest; you may survive even if you are dishonest. Which vocation offers so many options!

If I were to be born again, I would love to live the life of a civil servant all over again. Moreover, it would not be my father's decision but mine.

Abbreviations

ABDL	:	Activity Based Digital Learning
APL	:	Above Poverty Line
B. Ed	:	Bachelor in Education
BJD	:	Biju Janata Dal
BJP	:	Bharatiya Janata Party
BPL	:	Below Poverty Line
CAG	:	Comptroller and Auditor General of India
CBI	:	Central Bureau of Investigation
CBSE	:	Central Board of Secondary Education
CCI	:	Cabinet Committee on Investment
CCEA	:	Cabinet Committee on Economic Affairs
CIC	:	Central Information Commission
CII	:	Confederation of Indian Industries
CM	:	Chief Minister
CSS	:	Centrally Sponsored Scheme
CVC	:	Central Vigilance Commission
D.El.Ed	:	Diploma in Elementary Education
DFID	:	Department for International Development
DM	:	District Magistrate
ESIC	:	Employee State Insurance Corporation
FICCI	:	Federation of Indian Chambers of Commerce and Industry
FINO	:	Financial Inclusion Network & Operations Paytech Limited
IAS	:	Indian Administrative Service
IBWG	:	Inter Board Working Group
ILO	:	International Labour Organisation
IPS	:	Indian Police Service
JVC	:	Justice Verma Commission
LWE	:	Left Wing Extremism

MAS : Mandatory Affidavit System
MHRD : Ministry of Human Resource Development
MSTC : Metal Scrap Trading Corporation
NAAC : National Assessment and Accreditation Council
NCERT : National Council of Educational Research and Training
NCEUS : National Commission for Enterprises in the Unorganised Sector
NCTE : National Council for Teacher Education
NIC : National Informatics Centre
NREGS : National Rural Employment Guarantee Scheme
OPD : Outpatient Department
PA : Personal Assistant
PDS : Public Distribution System
PICUP : Pradeshiya Investment Corporation of Uttar Pradesh
PMG : Project Management Group
POS : Point of Sale
PROBE : Public Report on Basic Education
PSM : Pragat Shaikshanik Maharashtra
QCI : Quality Council of India
RSBY : Rashtriya Swasthya Bima Yojana
RTE : Right of Children to Free and Compulsory Education
SOP : Standard Operating Procedure
SSA : Sarva Shiksha Abhiyan
STQC : Standardisation Testing and Quality Certification
TEI : Teacher Education Institutions
TET : Teacher Eligibility Test
TPAs : Third-Party Administrators
UGC : University Grants Commission
UHIS : Universal Health Insurance Scheme
UIDAI : Unique Identification Authority of India
UPSIDC : Uttar Pradesh State Industrial Development Corporation